Transmission Difficulties

Transmission Difficulties

Franz Boas and Tsimshian Mythology

Ralph Maud

Talonbooks 2000

Talonbooks
#104—3100 Production Way
Burnaby, British Columbia, Canada V5A 4R4

Typeset in Garamond and printed and bound in Canada by Hignell Printing.

First Printing: June 2000

Talonbooks are distributed in Canada by General Distribution Services, 325 Humber College Blvd., Toronto, Ontario, Canada M9W 7C3; Tel.:(416) 213-1919; Fax:(416) 213-1917.

Talonbooks are distributed in the U.S.A. by General Distribution Services Inc., 4500 Witmer Industrial Estates, Niagara Falls, New York, U.S.A. 14305-1386; Tel.:1-800-805-1083; Fax:1-800-481-6207.

Canadä

The publisher gratefully acknowledges the financial support of the Canada Council for the Arts; the Government of Canada through the Book Publishing Industry Development Program; and the Province of British Columbia through the British Columbia Arts Council for our publishing activities.

Canadian Cataloguing in Publication Data

Maud, Ralph, 1928-
    Transmission difficulties

    Includes bibliographical references.
    ISBN 0-88922-430-7

    1. Boas, Franz, 1858-1942. 2. Tsimshian mythology. 3. Tsimshian Indians--Historiography. 4. Tate, Henry W. 5. Ethnology--North America--Historiography. 6. Ethnology--North America--Methodology. I.Title.

E99.T8M38 2000   306'.089'9741   C00-910138-1

Franz Boas in front of the house he had constructed at 230 Franklin Avenue in Grantwood, New Jersey, on the Palisades opposite Columbia University and readily accessible by the Fort Lee Ferry.

Photo courtesy of the American Philosophical Society.

The only known photograph of Henry Tate, left, "interpreter and assistant teacher," with Thomas Crosby, at the Mission school, Port Simpson.

Photo courtesy of the B.C. Archives and Records Service HP 10727.

Contents

Author's note

I acknowledge the generosity of the following depositories for making manuscripts and photographs available to me: (1) the Rare Books and Manuscripts Division of the Butler Library, Columbia University, New York; (2) Ethnology Division Library of the B.C. Provincial Museum, Victoria; (3) Canadian Centre for Folk Culture Studies, Ottawa; (4) University Archives, University of Washington, Seattle; (5) American Philosophical Society Library, Philadelphia; (6) Department of Anthropology, The American Museum of Natural History, New York; (7) Provincial Archives of British Columbia, Victoria; (8) B.C. Indian Language Project, Victoria; (9) The Wellcome Institute for the History of Medicine, London; (10) National Anthropological Archives, Smithsonian Institution, Washington, D.C.

I am indebted to several good friends and co-workers in the field, but because they could not possibly agree with the polemical tone of this book, I offer them the courtesy of not mentioning them by name.

Introduction

I come back to the *Tsimshian Mythology* volume once again and, as always, I am dismayed—no, outraged, really—at the charade that passes for scientific truth. I believe that in this enterprise Franz Boas has, for the sake of an intellectual chimera called "anthropological data," spoiled a great opportunity to add to humanistic knowledge. My purpose here, therefore, has to involve an exposé of sorry errors of judgment and commission in the collaboration between Boas and Henry Tate that produced a volume which has been generally prized. In the words of Melville Jacobs, *Tsimshian Mythology* is "monumental" and "prodigious":[1] it is not only an enormously large collection of one tribe's repertoire emanating from a most resourceful informant (Tate sent Boas two thousand pages of text between 1903 and 1913) but it also stands as the epitome of Boas's methodology in the categorization and analysis of myth (two-fifths of *Tsimshian Mythology* is devoted to a comparative study of myth motifs). This massive production has, however, not been subjected very much to the spotlight of critical inquiry. The Canadian, Marius Barbeau, was fearless in his *American Anthropologist* review in 1917, but nobody has been fearless on the U.S. side of the border.

The nearest anyone has come to saying "boo!" is Viola Garfield in her stern statement that the "collection, recording and publishing of myths and folktales demands certain responsibilities of the collector," that is, to explain fully what is happening at every point in the process. *Tsimshian Mythology*, in this light, is inadequate: "Documentation of the sources utilized by Mr. Tate, and of the amount of editing of them by himself and Dr. Boas would have been of great assistance, but it is lacking."[2] But even this criticism is protective. Sufficient documentation was available to Garfield in archives if she had really wanted to know how badly Boas had violated her principles of folklore collecting. For instance, a recorder must give us "any information on how the stories were obtained": "A direct request for a story may elicit quite a different response from that arising from other circumstances" (p. 28). We know from letters that Boas sometimes asked Tate for specific stories even though he does not divulge this in *Tsimshian Mythology*.

Garfield assumed a mask of calm common sense while delivering her deathblows to Boas's methodology. She herself had been a Ph.D. student with Boas in the 1930s and well knew whose defects she was mainly getting at when she talked vaguely about "scholars," "recorders" and "writers" in the field. How could she not be consciously undermining an essential tenet of Boas's when she declared: "for various reasons writers have neglected or hesitated to describe informants and interpreters. Yet narrators' personalities, sex, interests and experiences have an important influence on their selection of tales, how they select motifs and develop stories" (p. 27)? We would take this for granted today, but in 1953, apparently, it still needed to be said. And why? Because Boas had deliberately treated his informants as ciphers. It was necessary to his justifying folklore as data, data for tribal characteristics and for theories of diffusion. If all you got after a day's work with an informant was merely one person's view of things, that would not help very much; scientific data would be extremely elusive and require much more time and effort than Boas could spare for any one project when he had set himself the goal of covering everything. No, the individual, Boas decided, would have to stand for the whole tribe, nothing less. He erected this need into a rule of operation: informants have no personal identity. Finally, someone in 1953 was saying that this wouldn't do. Of course Garfield wasn't being that brave: Boas had been dead for ten years. And she could have laid the blame more squarely on his shoulders. She could have said, for example, "Why the hell didn't Boas tell us who Henry Tate was?"

The man with whom Boas exchanged letters over a ten-year period, from whom he bought invaluable texts by the page, whose work he depended on in order to register the inner life of a whole nation, Boas was content to refer to this person merely as "a full-blood Indian of Port Simpson, British Columbia": this in a preliminary publication of Tate stories, *Tsimshian Texts* (1912). In *Tsimshian Mythology* itself (1916) Boas doesn't even say that much by way of introduction. He thought it better to leave Tate faceless, a rounded mouth only, a zero through which the "Tsimshian" speak.

Boas actually knew plenty, more than we shall now ever know. Tate had sent him a whole letter about himself, an introductory letter containing his credentials. This letter is unfortunately lost, and we can only try in some rough fashion to reconstruct what it contained from the context in which it was written. Tate came on the scene in this wise. Boas wrote first to Arthur Wellington Clah of Port Simpson, 15 April 1903: "My friend, George Hunt, of Fort Rupert, Vancouver Island, writes me that you are very interested in preserving the traditions of your people."[3] We must pause here to note that this gambit in itself strains one's credulity. Clah was in reality the very last person to turn to for traditional Tsimshian mythology. He was certainly the most famous living Tsimshian, but famous for being the Rev. William Duncan's most zealous con-vert, saving that rabid Yorkshireman's life when the Chief Legaix of the time was very sensibly intending to do him in. (Duncan was apparently ringing the Sunday school bell in order to disrupt Tsimshian initiation ceremonies.)[4] In gratitude, the obnoxious Duncan gave him the Clah name and made him a monitor.

("Clah" is presumably the klah of Chinook jargon, meaning "escape, come into the light.") If George Hunt had known of Clah's Christian evangelicalism (and why didn't he?), he would hardly have suggested him as an enthnographic assistant. We can read in the Wellcome Library, London, Clah's manuscript journals with their "regular pious interjections"[5] and his illiterate "Reminiscences" of tribal legends (where Raven is Satan) and feel that it was, indeed, providential that Clah had just received a call to go off somewhere lay preaching when Boas's letter arrived inquiring if Clah wouldn't like "to join hands" with him "in preserving the history of the Tsimshian." The letter got passed on to Henry Wellington Tate, and the fiasco that Hunt had initiated was averted.

Because—and this is one of the chief things Boas did not tell us—Henry Tate was smart. Very smart. We have an advantage over Boas here in that a snapshot of a very smart-looking Tate has come to light. It is a group photograph of Rev. Thomas Crosby's mission school children and teachers in what must be the early 1880s, and the young man on the left, formally dressed but gracefully casual in his stance—one hand on the balustrade, the other held in repose at his jacket hem—is our Henry Tate, identified as "interpreter and assistant teacher."[6] Crosby was the great Methodist preacher of this coast, and no fool; he would not hire an assistant teacher out of charity. Another glimpse we get of Tate in this milieu is in a letter to the *Missionary Outlook* in 1894 penned by Tate and a friend, Samuel Bennett, which describes Crosby's Band of Christian Workers venturing with Captain William Oliver of the *Boscowitz* to proselytize outside Port Simpson, it being "the first time that we...have started out by ourselves to carry the Gospel."[7]

But Tate was no sectarian, and when William Ridley, the Episcopal Bishop of Caledonia (who arrived in Metlakatla from the Punjab in 1879), needed help with his translation of the Gospels into the Tsimshian language Tate was one of those called upon. At least we can assume his active engagement in that work. His total familiarity with the orthography Ridley devised for that purpose indicates it. Boas understood the situation immediately and in response to that first, missing letter of Tate's said in a reply of 13 May 1903: "The few lines of Zimshian [Boas here bowing to Ridley's usage] that you wrote in your letter are very pleasing to me, and I understand them well and can read your writing easily. I have myself the translations made by the Bishop of Caledonia with the help of Mrs. Morrison, whom I know well" (letter in American Museum of Natural History, AMNH). Perhaps Tate had mentioned Mrs. Morrison and the Gospels in his letter; in any case, his proficiency with Ridley's way of writing Tsimshian words was just not likely to have come to him by any other means. "No missionary can be dull among the Zimshian Indians," William Ridley wrote in his autobiography. "They have an alertness of mind and purpose which forbids stagnation."[8] One likes to think that the good bishop had Henry Tate in mind when he said this.

What else can be deduced about Tate's background? There is an arresting remark at the beginning of Boas's letter of 13 May 1903 that refers to something Tate must have mentioned in the missing letter.

> Mr. Henry Wellington Tate
> Port Simpson, B.C.
> Dear Sir.—
>
> I was very glad to receive your letter of May 2, and I am
> pleased to hear that you are willing to write down the
> history of the Zimshian. I shall be just as much pleased
> if you will do this as if your father would do it...

Arthur Wellington Clah was Tate's father? That should be something worth mentioning if you wanted to authenticate your otherwise anonymous informant. You couldn't get the number one man, but at least you got his son. That's something. Or maybe not? Boas thought not. He didn't mention it.

Settling Tate's antecedents would have saved us from what is at present a very tangled skein. A stigma was placed on Tate by Barbeau in his review of *Tsimshian Mythology* when he was explaining what he considered severe limitations in Tate's myth collecting. "He is not likely to have consulted many outside his own family members," says Barbeau (1917:553). "The fact that he himself belonged to the lower class (a Raven clan in the Gitzaxlel tribe, if we remember well) may not have made him *persona grata* with most of the chiefs—royal or others." Rather devastating this, and so casually stated. What if Barbeau was not remembering well? He is risking a carelessness bordering on defamation. He was, of course, relying here on his own informant William Beynon—who should have known what he was talking about, being Arthur Wellington Clah's daughter's son and thus, according to my reckoning, Tate's nephew! But curiouser yet, for Marjorie Halpin's definitive article "William Beynon, Ethnographer" states that "Beynon's mother's only surviving brother, Albert Wellington, held the high-ranking Niska Laxkibu name, Gusgain, which Beynon himself was later to assume" (Halpin 1978:142). Some of the inconsistencies (I'm not sure all) can be explained by an item in the "Tsimshian Society" section of *Tsimshian Mythology* under the sub-heading "Social Rank" where Boas is explaining the system of adoption permitted when a family might otherwise die out and he uses Tate himself as an illustration: "His own mother's father adopted him, and gave him the legal status of a sister's son, transmitting his name to him. While he is by birth a member of the Eagle group, he became then a member of the Gispawadweda, and henceforth could marry only a woman of the Wolf or Ganhada groups" (1916:500).[9] If it is Arthur Wellington Clah who is being referred to here as Tate's mother's father, then Tate and Beynon were brothers! This is obviously a problem that only someone well versed in Tsimshian lineage questions could untangle. But Marius Barbeau was such, and he should have tackled this adoption matter instead of just repeating Beynon's snobbish remarks. But then, how can one really blame Barbeau when this essential biographical information is hidden on p. 500, half way through an enormous volume? It should have been put up front as part of a full introduction to Henry Tate.

So should any and all pertinent evidence from Tate's first letter have been. Indeed, that first letter, in order for us to get the flavour of the man, should have been printed in full. Then we would not mind so much that the original was lost. As it is, it is simply annoying to see file after file of manuscript remains at the American Museum of Natural History, Columbia University, the American Philosophical Society and the Smithsonian Institution— much of it inconsequential—and this most interesting letter of all goes missing.[10]

I trust I have already said enough in this introduction to suggest how exasperating *Tsimshian Mythology* is because of all the opportunities lost. I will with some stubbornness persist until I fully reveal that this monumental book has feet of clay. At the same time, *Tsimshian Mythology* is truly prodigious and, with some effort of reevaluation, it might in the future be turned to good use in a way its caster could not—it is clear—imagine. The small book I have undertaken to write can only begin the process, which will of course have to be completed by scholars in full command of the Tsimshian language. The reason that someone like myself (not able to make such a claim) can proceed at all in this prolegomenon is in itself interesting. How can a mere English speaker propose to handle this material? The answer to this question leads directly into a consideration of another example of Boasian sleight of hand.

Chapter One

The first paragraph of Boas's preface to *Tsimshian Mythology* consists of three sentences, one of which is true:

> The following collection of Tsimshian myths was recorded during the last twelve years by Mr. Henry W. Tate, of Port Simpson, British Columbia, in Tsimshian, his native language. Mr. Tate died in April, 1914. The translation of the tales as here presented was made by me, based on a free interlinear rendering by Mr. Tate (1916:31).

The first sentence gives the impression that Tate "recorded" his tales by going out and asking knowledgable people to tell their stories in the traditional manner and taking down a text from their lips: the truth is quite contrary to this. The second sentence is true. The third sentence gives the impression that Boas translated these stories from Tate's Tsimshian aided by Tate's own English rendering: this is again what anyone would expect to have happened, but it patently did not.

The evidence that Tate wrote the stories in English—and then translated the English into Tsimshian interlinearly—is clear on every page of the manuscripts. Appendix A, "The History of

Porcupine," though included for later discussion, bears this out just as well as any. The English title comes first, and the first line of the story text is in English. But not only that: the English is always evenly spaced and neatly fills the lines up to the right hand margin, whereas the Tsimshian lines are irregular, sometimes spaced widely, sometimes cramped, in order to have the Tsimshian translation come directly underneath the appropriate English phrase. This may not be too noticeable on the first page of the story until the very bottom, where it is extremely evident in line 13 (someone, convenient for our purposes, numbered the manuscript lines). The English words, "Bear said. will you come in here," evenly fill the line; the Tsimshian translation is only four words, and dashes are used to pad the space. On the second page of the story, line 5 of the Tsimshian is very cramped, as is line 12; line 10, on the other hand, is spread out with a large space before "du'du'uh" so that the bear-talk can come in line with its counterpart above. Similarly, lines 4 and 8 on the next page. And so on, throughout. The English telling comes first and the Tsimshian is a translation of the English.

This is not what was supposed to happen. The primary text was supposed to be some old story-teller's Tsimshian words; here it is Tate's English. Hence, the authenticity of the result of this process is undermined. It must have horrified Boas to see this happening, once he noticed. He let 450 pages in six batches sent by Tate between Sept 1903 and May 1904 go by before he woke up to the damage and tried to apply some control. "It also seems to me," he wrote Tate in a letter of 22 May 1905, "that you write the English first, and the Indian afterwards between the lines. I should like it much better to have the stories told in just the same way as they are told by your people" (letter AMNH). He asks him point blank to "write your Tsimshian first, just as your old people are in the habit of telling the stories, and then to write the English between the lines." Boas reiteraites this in the same words in a postscript to the letter. Tate in subsequent letters did not acknowledge the problem, so Boas in a letter of 26 September 1905 asks him again "to write the Zimshian first, and the English afterwards, and to give it as near as you can in the words of the wise old men" (letter AMNH). Tate never responded to Boas on this question, and the evidence is that during the whole of his ten years of sending bilingual material to Boas, he continued the practise of writing the story first in English and filling in the Tsimshian line afterward. He was, in short, writing these stories in English.[11]

Let us turn from Boas's discomfiture for a moment to speculate about why Tate would persist in this way. One reason may have been purely economic. In his letter of 23 June 1903 Boas offered Tate 15¢ a page: "You can, I presume, easily write five pages or more an hour, so that this would equal 75 cents an hour pay" (letter AMNH). We have ventured that Tate was a smart man and venture further that he said to himself: "So I can 'easily' write five pages an hour, can I? Well, yes, if I do it the way that is easiest for me." But why should English be the easier language to write in? Whatever stories he had heard in his life and remembered, whatever stories he went and asked people for, whatever thinking he was doing to put them into shape, all was in the Tsimshian language. Yet when he put pen to paper it was the English that came out first. There would likely be something habitual about it, and it is safe to speculate that in helping Bishop Ridley turn the English of the Gospels into Tsimshian, that direction of translation had become ingrained. It might have felt unnatural to do it the other way. Dell Hymes has proposed (in a personal communication, 20 July 1985) that Tate's basic relationship to Boas, the university professor, would be another factor. English would be Tate's language of literacy and "perhaps the task set by Boas seemed to him first and foremost a literacy task, therefore to be done in the language of literacy, with the writing of Tsimshian a more difficult task."[12] Dennis Tedlock, from his experiences in the field, has discovered a general rule: "When the informant is bilingual but untrained by previous linguists, he will always try to summon up the investigator's humanness at this point, wanting to tell the story in English...so that the investigator will *understand*" (1977:509). In fact, in his very first letter Boas made a point of saying that he did not know the Tsimshian language very well. Tate might possibly have had in the back of his mind that it would be helping Boas to have the stories told in English rather than in a language he couldn't understand as easily.

There is another factor that Boas should have anticipated, but didn't. In the specific instruction he gave Tate in a letter of 23 June 1903 he said he was willing to engage himself to take 1000 pages "written in Zimshian, with translation between the lines in the manner of my Naas River book" (letter AMNH). When Boas first wrote to Arthur Wellington Clah he enclosed most of the Northwest Coast texts that had been published up to that time, including *Tsimshian Texts (Nass River Dialect)* (1902). This move was fraught with predictable dangers.

Appendix B reproduces the first few pages of the stories Boas himself collected from Nishka speakers in Kinkolith at the mouth of the Nass river in late 1894. Boas thought that sending these samples would be an efficient way to train informants whom he could not reach in person. But when Tate looked at these pages, what was he confronted with right away? A story written out in English. On the lower part of the page there was some funny phonetic wording completely opaque to him.[13] Then, interlinearly, some equally funny pidgin English. This was the opposite of a training manual; it was a positive deterrent. Only the free English rendering would appear at all usable. If Tate was to do his work "in the manner of" *Tsimshian Texts* (1902) as he had been asked, he might well feel that what Boas wanted, *at least*, was a story that they could both read. That, at least. It would be natural to take Boas's instructions in this regard as supporting his inclination—his habit from previous translating work—to use first and foremost a readable English narrative, and let the interlinear line be a simple sort of Tsimshian to match the simple English.

Since Tate was completely unresponsive and unchanging on this interlinear question, Boas did not reiterate his pleas after the 22 May 1905 letter, probably reckoning he was getting *something* for his money. But he was not getting "the words of the wise old men," so he had an authenticity problem. Or he thought he had. He could not see that Tate's way of doing it might prove to be a uniquely interesting stepping-stone between the oral and literary modes, and that, filtered as they are through the mind of a talented writer of some sensibility, these narratives might gain from the process. No, Boas could only see it in terms of a problem, and his solution was to pretend there was no problem. He had an English line and a Tsimshian line, didn't he? So let's just pretend that the Tsimshian line came first. In the opening paragraph of the preface to *Tsimshian Mythology* quoted above, Boas pretends that Tate recorded these texts in his native language. Not only that, but also that he himself translated them from the Tsimshian.

There is evidence that Boas made serious attempts at translating Tate's Tsimshian. The markings Boas made on the first fourteen pages of Tate's "The History of Tkaumshim" (Columbia pp. 365-379) indicate he was trying to do a word for word translation of the Tsimshiam lines interlinearly, but there are many gaps where he was apparently unclear about the grammatical construction. And when he starts again with the same passage on a new sheet of paper, putting the Tsimshian line first in the way he wished Tate had done and trying to translate from the Tsimshian alone, he stops the attempt before he gets to the bottom of the page (manuscript in American Philosophical Society APS). He tries the same thing with what Tate called "The History of the wild beast Meeting" (Columbia p. 286) and what Boas, translating Tate's Tsimshian title literally, titled in the manuscript (APS) "Story of animals of country" (published 1916:106-108 as "The Meeting of the Wild Animals"). But only two pages survive.

It is hard to prove a negative. Perhaps Boas did translate all the two thousand pages and the translation is no longer extant. But this conclusion is highly unlikely, given what we know he did when he came to publish the first batch of Tate's work. "In written texts, inaccuracies of construction creep in easily," Boas remarked in his introduction to *Tsimshian Texts* (1912). "I should have preferred a revision of the texts with Mr. Tate, but this was not feasible"

(1912:69). In other words, he could not really read Tate's Tsimshian, not all of it anyway, without consulting him on various points. He was not planning to be out in British Columbia for a while, but he felt the need to get some of this Tsimshian work into print. Urgency is the mother of ingenuity; Boas found a solution closer at hand.

Boas got wind of the presence of a certain Archie Dundas, "a full-blood Tsimshian from New Metlakatla, Alaska" (1912:67) resident at the Carlisle Indian School in Pennsylvania, and he brought him up to New York City for the month of April 1908. Dundas was asked to read aloud Tate's Tsimshian sentences, and Boas took them down afresh phonetically as though he were in the field, exercising that great skill he had with languages. This way any inadequacies in Tate's written Tsimshian would be remedied. Dundas would know what Tate was trying to say, and would speak it correctly. Thus there would be an accurate and translatable text. Boas was not perfectly happy with the result: "The phonetic analysis of Tsimshian is not quite adequate, because all the material at my disposal was read to me once only by a single man" (1912:254). In this department Boas set himself high standards; I think we can assume, despite this caveat, that his work with Dundas had produced a linguistically clear text.

But more authentic? Hardly. We seem to have taken a step still further away from the "words of the wise old men." "In the following texts," says Boas in the introduction to *Tsimshian Texts* without telling us why, "the grammatical forms given by Archie Dundas have been given preference over those of Mr. Tate, who tends to substitute the forms peculiar to direct discourse for those characteristic of indirect discourse" (1912:68). (I must admit to not understanding that sentence at all, even when Boas gives three supposed explanatory illustrations.) "In other cases Mr. Tate uses the indicative where Dundas prefers the subjunctive" (1912:69). This I understand, but I don't see why Dundas's preference is, in fact, preferable. "Apparently some slight differences in dialect have developed between the Tsimshian of the older people who staid in

British Columbia [i.e. Tate], and the younger generation who migrated to Alaska [i.e. Dundas]" (1912:67). All right, but then why bother with Dundas? All these statements suggest that Dundas's rescension has distorted the original. It was up to Boas to step forward and tell us why, in spite of the distortions, it had to be done this way. He does not do so, I suppose, because the truth about the inadequacy of Tate's Tsimshian writing of his own language would give the game away. It would undermine what this whole project was based upon: Tate's authority as a transmitter of authentic oral narratives. So Boas tells us something of what the Dundas presence has produced, but he has soft-pedalled the reasons for having him there at all.

Boas also hides another important fact: that in translating Dundas's Tsimshian, he categorically refused to utilize Tate's English line. A few illustrations will show how this stubbornness serves the reader badly. The facsimile of Tate's "The History of Porcupine" from the Columbia manuscripts presented in Appendix A gives us the first few lines of English as follows:

> While the time in the Fall when all the animals went
> into their Dens, also the great Grizzly Bear sat into his
> own Den for Winter sleep, and the great rain descended
> and therefore the drops of water in the great Grizzly
> Bear's den, and his fur is full of wets and he was
> disappoint as long as the rain.

Tate's Tsimshian lines read by Dundas and translated by Boas give us:

> It was when it was fall, and all the animals were in their
> towns. Then Great-Grizzly-Bear was also in his town
> because it was mid-winter. Then rain came down and
> dropped into the den [town] of Great-Grizzly-Bear,
> whose fur was wet; and he was much annoyed on
> account of the long rain (1912:237).

Let me say up front—and this is almost invariably true throughout—I like Tate's English style better than Boas's. The diction always has more vitality. Isn't "his fur is full of wets" infinitely more enjoyable as a phrase than "whose fur was wet"? I do not think I have fallen here into the trap of sentimentalizing the "siwash." Tate was a much better writer than Boas's presentations of his work have allowed us to appreciate.

But, it is more than a question of style. To look at some details in the above passages: the Tsimshian word "ts!ap" usually means "town" (see the vocabulary 1912:271), so Boas translates it as "town" when it occurs twice in the first couple of lines. When it appears a third time and cannot mean anything other than "den" Boas puts "den [town]" and uses "den" thereafter. What was the point of giving the translation as "town" at all when Tate indicated in his English that he meant "den" from the start? Boas is just being silly, acting like a rigorous scientific linguist in a totally misplaced fashion.

This touch of officious superiority would be negligible if it did not herald worse. The story proceeds as per Boas (1912:237):

> While he was sitting there, behold! Porcupine went
> towards him. As he passed the door of Great-Grizzly-
> Bear's den, Grizzly-Bear said, "Come in, friend! Come
> in, friend! You shall eat with me." Therefore Porcupine
> entered the den of Grizzly-Bear.
>
> Then Great-Grizzly-Bear made a great fire. He took
> little Porcupine, tied his feet and hands, and put him by
> the side of the fire. Then Porcupine's back was burned
> by the fire.

Now to compare Tate's original English (Appendix A):

> And while he was there, Behold a Porcupine coming
> along. As she passed the door of great Grizzly Bear Den,
> that Grizzly Bear said, will you come in here my friend,

> I will sup with you. Therefore the Porcupine turn in the
> great Grizzly Bear's Den. Then the Grizzly Bear make a
> large fire. Then he caught the poor Porcupine, and bind
> her foot and hand, and put her near the fire and burnt
> her back fur with fire.

Porcupine is female! The bear's sadism takes on quite a different
weight and tone. There was apparently nothing in Dundas's
rendering that indicated Porcupine was a "she," so Boas pig-head-
edly made her a male in spite of Tate's intention, which presumably
reflects the tradition.

We now reach a major challenge to the methodology. Where
Dundas found Tate's Tsimshian impossible to fathom, surely he
could take a peek at Tate's English to see what he intended the
Tsimshian to say? Apparently not. It would cast doubt on the pri-
macy of the Tsimshian text to do such a thing. Better, it seems, to
declare the Tsimshian words "unintelligible" (1912:236) and
denote the gap in sense by means of question marks (1912:237):

> Great-Grizzly-Bear said, "? ? ? du-u, du-u!" Thus said
> Great-Grizzly-Bear. "I shall do so," said Porcupine. "O
> chief! untie my bands, then I will do what you say."

This is quite a scene: the tortured female says she will do anything
the big bear wants! No, it's not what you think. Any bear knows
very well that a porcupine has the special skill of making the
weather change to induce frost. Better snow than all this damn
rain, thinks the Grizzly. That's why he invites her in and is tortur-
ing her. Everybody knows that. But Boas, if he knows it (and of
course he does), cannot allow himself to put it down, stymied
because he cannot work out the syntax of the Tsimshian that
Dundas is getting from Tate. Tate is quite clear in his English:

> Then the great Grizzly Bear have said to Porcupine,
> while he was burnt her back fur, Make frost your little

unsightly animal. du'du'uh says the great Grizzly Bear.
Yes. I will do said the Porcupine...

Boas's rigidity gets all the more ludicrous as this stage business is repeated twice more in the story. The second time it is: "make frost you little ugly Porcupine;" and the third time: "Make a frost you little unsightly animal." (I have encircled these three occurrences in the Appendix A pages.) In all three cases Boas gives us the blank "? ? ?" How can it possibly be of any help to anybody to say that Tate is unintelligible on these three occasions? It is well known that when you get verbal tags or jigs of this kind in a story the words are going to be of the most archaic order. The antiquity of these elements should be relished, not banished. Tate knows what this "Old Tsimshian" means, and so does Boas, even if he has to pretend not to. I cannot express how annoyed I am with Boas for having spoiled this story for everyone who has tried to read it in *Tsimshian Texts*. The work has all to be done over again. The tales have to be rescued from Boas's leaden hand.[14]

There is more. The song, with Tate's musical notation (see Appendix A), must again be of great antiquity. One would certainly expect that it would be the Tsimshian words that would fit the rhythm of the music. Possibly in this case the Tsimshian words came first. In any case, the intimacy between musical phrase, Tsimishian chant and English translation is something that should get the best attention of an expert mind—someone like Boas. How does Boas respond to this challenge? First he decides that this is one instance when he will break his rule not to consult Tate's English and quotes the two lines (1912:239):

"As I walk at the foot of a beautiful green mountain, All
the stars of heaven are glittering as the north wind
clears the sky."

Boas has not transcribed Tate's words precisely, but perhaps the differences are negligible. The point is, Porcupine is singing a sacred song that will produce frosty weather; the lines are beautifully appropriate. Presumably the Tsimshian lines should give us the same, or the equivalent. But Boas's footnote indicates he is having difficulty (1912:239):

> The translation of the song is not clear. So far as the words are intelligible, they may be translated as follows: "Around the foot of the door goes ? ? ? Fog is around, stars are around the head waters of the Skeena River and the head waters of Nass River."

Apart from noting that the words for the Skeena and Nass rivers appear to be crossed out in Tate's manuscript, I cannot myself add much to clear up this problem. But Boas should have worked on it a little harder; he should have asked Dundas some serious questions about what Tate is trying to do here, how the Tsimshian words might offer what Tate puts down in his English, why the whole thing might make good imaginative sense. We do not know that he didn't; but it looks as though he just put down what Dundas gave him at first try in all its garbled glory and then added, making Tate look like a fool for not being able to translate his own Tsimshian properly: "The translation given above is the interpretation of the song given by Mr. Tate" (1912:239 footnote). We have a similar situation with the song in the companion story in *Tsimshian Texts*, "Story of Porcupine and Beaver." Porcupine is again singing her song to change the weather. She must have two songs, for this one is quite different (and thus, unfortunately, does not offer a comparison), as can be seen from the facsimile below from Columbia MS p. 766:

First the lightning from the north burns the water; then the north wind freezes it. We seem to get only the first part here. The repeated refrain in Tate's English is "They are burning, they are of heaven." This is associated with "my dearest children." It does not make sense in the ordinary way; we should not expect it to in a children's chant, any more than we understand why the cow jumped over the moon.[15] "We ever used those two songs," wrote Tate enclosing them to Boas on the 7th of February, 1908, "if we want to have a good weather, and we sang these songs" (letter Columbia). This puts the songs, and probably the stories also, into perspective: they were things Tate knew well from childhood and he is probably writing them down without recourse to informants. In any case, this nice bit of information from a letter is something that in Boas's methodology it was thought best to keep from the readers of the published story.

All in all, my contention is that these two Porcupine stories have "suffered in translation," as the saying goes. Further examples: "Bear" in line 6 of 1912:227 should be "Beaver." On p. 231 Boas/Dundas has Beaver saying, "I am always alive," when Tate's English says, "I am still alive." On p. 235 Boas/Dundas have it that "Porcupine tried to cure himself" while Tate's English says "the

Porcupine tried to get fresh air." These are all little things but they add up. One final example: Boas/Dundas (1912:239) have the abused Porcupine escaping with the threat: "I have reason to be ashamed of you, great strong Grizzly-Bear. Don't say anything when the ice comes to you." Tate's English has much more punch: "You big ugly great power Grizzly Bear, don't say anything if you frozen to dead in your Den" (Columbia pp. 755-56 Appendix A). There is no question which of these is preferable. The contrast in vitality between Tate and Boas here, and everywhere, makes one feel confident that Tate's English is the best text for the enjoyment of these tales as the "old wise men's" audience would have enjoyed them. Boas, in presenting a selection of these texts in 1912, should have tried to get as close to Tate's English as possible instead of using Dundas as a means of removing himself as far as possible from it.

When questioning the reliability of *Tsimshian Texts* (1912) as a whole we have to extrapolate from the two Porcupine stories, for, in the case of the other texts, Tate's manuscript pages are missing from the Columbia University deposit. "The Story of Asdi-wal," "Story of Gunaxnesemgad," "Gauo," and "Story of the Deluge"— these are among the most substantial and important myth artefacts of the Tsimshian that remain to us; the lack of Tate's originals is therefore especially disappointing. We have no way of checking into what errancies the Boas/Dundas detours have taken them; we have lost forever Tate's vigorous inimitable diction. Again, much anger that Boas should have allowed these stories in particular to disappear: I do not think that this disaster occurred after these papers left Boas's control.[16] The published versions are tarnished by uncertainty. The last sentence of "Story of the Porcupine" (1912:241) is not in Tate's version at all; it is a complete misreading by Dundas. How many times did such a thing happen in the course of these longer texts? We will probably never know.

When Archie Dundas went home to Alaska, Boas had no one else conveniently placed to turn to. In any case the circuitous process that had produced the bilingual text of the slender 1912 volume was tremendously time-consuming, and, if Boas were to fulfill his ambition of getting all of Tate's hundreds of manuscript pages into the record as data, he would have to cut some corners. He decided to use Tate's English after all and just knock it into shape. That's why the statement in the preface of *Tsimshian Mythology* is so deceiving: "The translation of the tales as here presented was made by me, based on a free interlinear rendering by Mr. Tate" (1916:31). Strictly speaking, there was no translation as such involved. Tate was not translating from the Tsimshian and neither was Boas. However, considering the 1912 fiasco and our conclusion that it would have been better to stay with Tate's English, we can only feel that Boas's subsequent decision to stay with Tate's English is a step in the right direction.

That having been said, we still have to put up with the stolid standard English that a well-trained nineteenth century German speaker had acquired. So the *Tsimshian Mythology* stories still suffer somewhat in "translation," and it is perhaps just as well that Boas did not spend too much time polishing his periods. We deduce that his method, generally, was to dictate to a stenographer. The name for "hail" in the story "The Deluge" is twice printed as "Living Eyes" (1916:347) instead of the "living Ice" of Tate's manuscript (Columbia pp. 587-88). The form "Living Eyes" could only have come from someone mishearing Boas's accent. He could hardly have written it himself with Tate in front of him, though clearly he overlooked it in proofreading.[17] From this and other details we conclude that Boas revised at great speed to produce a volume of quick cosmetic "improvements" of Tate's English lines.

"The Deluge" can be used to give an idea, at random, of the kind of tidying up this was. For one thing, Boas has shortened Tate's title, "The History of the world's Flood." Since there is nothing Noah-like about this story, any change of title should have taken us further away from Genesis rather than, with the emotion-filled "Deluge," towards it. The story is essentially about how someone became a shaman with the vision and power to lead the

Tsimshian nation from their mountainous stronghold to a totally new life as a coastal people. The story begins inland, in the long-ago (Columbia p. 584):

> Almost at the end of our grantfathers lives at Skeena as
> I mansion on the other history which we named Park or
> plain Village, and most of the people was very clevers
> they are handsome hunts, brave in war and so on. So on
> that days some hunters wents away from their homes
> to-ward the sun rise, soon they got along side a great
> Lake which the named very oldest Lake...

From the above Boas produced the following (1916:346):

> At the end of our ancestors' time the people lived on
> Skeena River, as I have told in another story, in a place
> named Prairie Town; and most of the people were
> clever, good hunters, and brave warriors. One day some
> hunters left their home and went toward the east. They
> came to a great lake named Lake Of The Beginning...

"Lake Of The Beginning:" I do not know where Boas got that one. "Prairie Town" is the old Temlaham: Archie Dundas told Boas it was translated "village on prairie" (1912:267, 243), and he stuck to that. Tate says the hunters are "handsome." Boas will only have them as "good." Boas says "east" for Tate's "sun rise." There is no need for these changes. Tate sent this story to Boas on 18 March 1905 along with "The Feast of the Mountain Goats." Boas could have been a little helpful and indicated that that was the other story referred to. Rather than make any such connection, he separated them in *Tsimshian Mythology* by two hundred pages.

Later, in one instance, Boas is a little too helpful. Two shamans come along in a canoe. He has Tate saying: "We call these her-maphrodites" (1916:348). What Tate wrote was (Columbia p. 592): "those shamans we call 'mans half women' or half-men."

Boas reckons he knows what Tate means and wants us to be sure. Indeed, when he uses the word "hermaphrodites" in his summary of this story in the notes (1916:862), Boas adds one of the rare footnotes of this volume: "Probably homosexuals are meant."

A cautious footnote, too. These little touches are the hallmark of misplaced meticulousness. I believe that Boas was not truly careful, only blindly meticulous. He gives pedantry a bad name. Hence, the nagging that is going on here. It is one of the aims of this book to prove just how uncaring Boas was most of the time. His reputation for accuracy turns out to be quite undeserved. Dennis Tedlock has called Boas's work "patient stenographic drudgery in the name of science" (Tedlock 1977:515). But Tedlock does not know the worst: that the "drudgery" is, in my experience of it, ill-conceived and full of careless errors. We cannot allow Boas even the noble name of drudge.

Let us watch him destroying this story "The Deluge" as he has others. The essence of the plot is an economic crisis which leaves the Tsimshian vulnerable to starvation; it is the vision of an "ever-living fish" which sustains them in their exodus to the sea. This fish turns out to be the halibut, and it is given mythic proportions in Tate's telling of it (Columbia p. 594):

> So these Shaman lied down on one side the fire he ask
> his friends to covering him with ceder bark mat, and he
> stard his supernaturals song [Tate gives the song] before
> he stard to sing and Thus he said, ever living fish, ever
> living fishs, my supernatural told me were ever-living
> fishs was now.

Boas, for reasons best known to himself (for I cannot fathom it), changes Tate's "ever-living fish" to "every living fish" (1916:349), giving this as the song:

Every living fish, every living fish,
My supernatural power told me where every living fish
is now.

And he omits Tate's next sentence which is essential for understanding the motivation in the plot (Columbia p. 594):

So we must go to where them fish was least we died
with starvation if we still abide in this old Village then
we shall die in starving.

Boas simply misses this sentence out. Not purposefully. Carelessly. It's a bad business, because without survival stressed in this way, what we see, in Boas's telling, is a demented shaman chanting over and over "every living fish" and "pointing with his finger down river" (1916:349). This story is epic: the fate of a nation is at stake. Boas garbles it.

With reference to *Tsimshian Mythology* as a whole, what is perhaps more annoying than the page after page of monotone that Boas's sensibility has imposed on Tate is the pretence that the creation of this monotony has all taken a great deal of effort and discrimination. Most notable are the occasions when Boas deliberately allows us to get the impression that he is translating from the Tsimshian. For instance, a Tsimshian word is left untranslated in the sentence, "The child wants to have a *gisox*" (1916:75); and a footnote explains: "The meaning of this word is unknown to me.—F.B." The impression is that Boas is translating along and doing all right, and then he comes to a difficult word and has to admit his ignorance. The fact is he has been following Tate's English, and then he comes to, "The child want to have a gishokt" (Columbia p. 439). It seems from the context to be a particular part of a seal that Tate has a Tsimshian word for, but no English equivalent. It is strictly true that "the meaning of this word is unknown" to Boas, but, in saying that, he is giving the appearance of translating all the rest.

Not only is Boas not translating Tate's Tsimshian, but on one occasion he refuses to consult it when it would be useful to do so, to get rid of the question mark in the following sentence: "The garment was full of the foam(?) of living persons" (1916:266). The Columbia manuscripts reveal what the trouble is. Tate had written "form" (p. 269), which would be an eminently suitable word in that context, but he then changed the "r" to "a" to make it "foam," which is so metaphoric in the phrase "foam of living persons" that Boas was constrained to question it. But the word Tate used in the Tsimshian line is "gapa," which is "wave" (see "gab" in the glossary to *Tsimshian Texts* p. 280); so there is no question at all that the word is "foam."

A similar example is Boas's footnoting "translation uncertain" in respect to the following sentence (1916:200): "Then the chief of the Spring Salmon saw the net of the great shaman on one side of the canyon, and stretching to the other side." Since the text is not a translation, what can Boas possibly mean? In the margin of the manuscript of this passage (Columbia p. 677) we see Boas's question mark. What is the problem? The sentence seems clear enough: "Then the chief of spring salmon saw the net of great sorcerer reaching on one side canyon and the part on the other side." In other words, there is no way for the spring salmon to get through without being caught in the net that reaches all the way across the canyon. The area of uncertainty here would seem to be extremely narrow. Boas does not specify which part of the sentence worries him; we presume it must be the phrase "stretching to" which he substitutes for Tate's awkward "the part." But if he looked at Tate's Tsimshian word—and I'm not saying he never did—he would have found "wagait," which he would have remembered that he had glossed previously as "completing an action entirely" (1912:259). So there is no problem here: "stretching to the other side", in the context of setting a net across a river, is quite satisfactory. Nothing uncertain about it. And yet there's the footnote: "Translation uncertain." Is it possible that the problem is—no, it couldn't be, could it? yet I believe it is—that Boas could not read Tate's handwriting for the word "part?" (It does look a bit like something that rhymes with "part.") If it is true that he couldn't read, or couldn't understand, the word "part," then only a totally misplaced scrupulousness would lead him to confess that the "translation" is "uncertain." Here, a difficulty with Tate's English has been elevated to a translation crux. There may be some other explanation, but, whatever it might be, this footnote is definitely misleading in that it gives the impression that the rest of this enormous volume, which is not a translation, has been translated without uncertainty.

Chapter Two

Boas wants us to know that, in one respect, Tate's work is not entirely authentic: "Mr. Tate felt it incumbent upon himself to omit some of those traits of the myths of his people that seem inappropriate to us, and there is no doubt that in this respect the tales do not quite express the old type of Tsimshian traditions" (1916:31). Boas could not quite bring himself to mention the word "sex;" but that is what he was getting at. He knew the sexually explicit material usually found in a ribald classic such as "Txamsen makes a Girl Sick and then Cures Her" (1916:81-84). Everyone knows what Raven intentions are when he arranges for a chief's daughter to be sick so that he can pose as a shaman to "cure" her. We all understand what is going on under the cedar bark mat that is covering Raven and the girl. So when Tate does not tell the story with the traditional degree of coarseness, Boas feels justified to state in his notes: "Evidently this incident is very much toned down" (1916:722). Tate, the accusation is, was betraying the tradition by an act of self-censorship (Columbia p. 471):

> Tkamshim ask and said bring up to me a ceder bark
> mat. Then they brought to him mat. He took it and
> spread it over the princess to cover her. He went also
> under it with the girl he touch the wound and had said

cure on under right ribs, so it was. Then the Chief was
very glad for his daughter was healed from her hurt.
Then he fed Tkamshim of all kinds of food.

Tate's premise is that food is uppermost in Raven's mind in
concocting this stratagem—and that is certainly true to character.
But all it takes is a wink and Tate's telling is as salacious as any.
Could he not be depending on what everybody knows: Raven
would not refuse a sexual encounter if it came to him while he was
honestly engaged in pursuing gluttony? For Boas, Tate has simply
not done his job unless the sex is there in all its coarseness. It is the
usual business: Indians are coarse, and it is not possible that some
story-tellers might be a little subtle, with a touch of irony perhaps.

Individual differences are not to be thought possible. If a story-
teller is not coarse, it cannot have anything to do with personal sen-
sitivity; it is that missionaries have curbed the natural brutishness.
"Christian influences are evidently very strong among all tribes of
northern British Columbia, and a study of the collection of tales
recorded by Doctor Swanton among the Haida and Tlingit shows
also very clearly that the coarseness of their tales has been very
much toned down" (1916:31). There are trends, and our Mr. Tate
is an instance of a trend. End of story.

Or perhaps the problem could be Boas himself. He states in the
preface that he has had "the personal experience that informants
were reluctant to express themselves freely in the traditional form,
being impressed by the restrictions of what we call proper and
improper" (1916:31). People usually know immediately who they
can tell an off-colour joke to. Melville Jacobs, in his brilliantly
insightful essay on Boas's "Folklore" in a festschrift volume
(1959:126-27) suggests that "obscenity was too distasteful to per-
mit him to make inquiries about sexual components of stories.
One cannot suppose that he enjoyed slang or primitive music; he
felt both were rather crude... The austere visitor probably mingled
politely with the natives, but with some discomfort..." Jacobs's
remarks strike one as intuitively precise. Tate never met Boas, so

did not have the benefit of seeing his body language, but letters can be revealing. Sending the first batch of Raven stories with a letter of 7 February 1907, Tate certainly seems to be testing Boas, feeling that he'd better see what the man is made of (letter at Columbia):

> many more Tkamshim's acts is not written down on my history that which you have for it is a very bad things so I did not put them down on my whole history For we are a live in the christian life, but I have some more different histories are better ones than those...

Tate is saying, shall I go on? Can you stand the heat? Boas's reply was very predictable, and has been held up as a model of what to say in these circumstances. George W. Stocking, Jr. printed it in full in *A Franz Boas Reader: The Shaping of American Anthropology, 1883-1911* (1989:124) as a key document, and we do likewise here:[18]

Mr. HENRY W. TATE,   March 28, 1907
Port Simpson, B.C.
MY DEAR MR. TATE,

> I was very glad to receive the 75 pages of the Tkamsum story, which you had the kindness to send me. I enclose in this letter a money-order for $15. As you will see, I have raised the pay to twenty cents a page instead of 15 cents, and I hope that this will be agreeable to you. I trust now that you will be willing to go on, and that I may look forward to some more matter in the near future.

> I was very much interested in reading what you have written, but you must allow me to say one thing. You write in your letter that you have omitted some of the

stories which to you and to me seem very improper; but if we want to preserve for future times a truthful picture of what the people were before they advanced to their present condition, we ought not to leave out anything that shows their ways of thinking, even though it should be quite distasteful to us.

It is just the same as with some of the horrid customs of olden times, like dog-eating and man-eating. You have no reason to be ashamed of what the people did in olden times, before they knew better: but if we want to give a truthful account of what there was, we ought not to be ashamed or afraid to write it down. I hope, therefore, that you may be willing to overcome your reluctance to write nasty things, since they belong to the tales that were told by your old people. For our purpose it is all-essential that whatever we write should be true, and that we should not conceal anything. You will recall that you promised also the story of Sucking-Intestines (Namomhat). I hope you will find time to write it to me, and to let me know how it is related to the Tkamsum story.

Yours very sincerely,

[Franz BOAS]

"Ah, as I thought" (we can imagine Henry Tate saying to himself), "this Boas hates Tsimshian culture, really hates it. He wants to know all the details so that he can say how disgusted he is." One can see how wary such a letter might cause the recipient to feel. It has the air of being tremendously well-intentioned, but, as Boas takes aim with such phrases as "the horrid customs of olden times," it backfires and blackens his face. "Before they knew better," indeed; it is so high-minded as to be quite unprofessional. It disqualifies Boas as an anthropologist, which I define as an ardent admirer of the way things are and were. An anthropologist courts experiences of all kinds and does not defame other people's sincerities. If one cannot identify with ethnic necessities—even the necessity of "ethnic cleansing," say, and the joy of it—then one had better turn elsewhere than anthropology for a career. A classicist has to put up with the fact that Odysseus on his return to Ithaca killed, in revenge, 108 suitors and, in cold blood, 12 maidservants who had fraternized with them. This was, to that society, an act of honour, justice, a reassertion of regal power; it is the kernel of Homer's thoughts on kingship. If you cannot glory with Odysseus here you cannot be a classicist. You cannot be a classicist only when it suits you. There are certain things that the field is defined by: Odysseus' homecoming slaughter is one of them. Northwest Coast anthropology is defined by head-hunting warfare, the cheating gluttony of the trickster, and the lineage boasting in the interminable garage sales called potlatches. If you cannot get into this sort of stuff, then quit. Don't preach about how superior we are now because we go to church and have better manners these days.

Or perhaps Boas was being professional. Anthropologists have been known to "agree" with informants they suspect may be a bit straightlaced, and who have come to believe that the old ways were outrageous. Maybe Boas's letter was a pose adopted in response to clues he thought he was getting from Tate. Maybe he was faking a like-mindedness in order to get more out of him: the means justifying the end of preserving "for future times a truthful picture."

I believe it was both things. Boas was genuinely horrified by savage practices, but he prided himself on being a professional who shouldn't be. Therefore, when he wrote about being disgusted, he was, in his own mind, faking it as a device for evoking more information about things that in his soul he did not really want to know about. It is my opinion that Boas was so ethically mixed up that one should hesitate to believe any single thing he said. If Tate was as smart as we have imagined, then he would harbour deep suspicions of this voice coming through in such a preachy letter.

He would have to be careful. Total disclosure was being requested, but the accompanying message was that it would not be liked. Better, on the whole, to tone it down.

Tone it down Tate did. But what is really amazing is that despite the earnest plea in the letter that "it is all-essential that whatever we write should be true, and that we should not conceal anything," even Tate's toned-down versions were too much for Boas. In presenting Tate's stories to the public a great deal more bowdlerization was apparently necessary.

For example, "Burning Leggings and Burning Snowshoes" (1916 #30) includes a scene of sexual entrapment. A jealous first wife wants to get the second wife into trouble, and the visit of the second wife's brother offers an opportunity. She sees that he has some red ochre face paint and sends a slave girl to tell him that she wants some of it and, according to the Tate manuscript (Columbia p. 327), "will lie with him on behind our house." Boas has it that she promised "to meet him behind the house" (1916:217). The young man refuses and the wife sends the slave girl again for some of his "red sand:" "tell him that I want to lie with him outside, right now" (Columbia p. 328). Boas tones this down again to "she would meet him outside right away" (1916:217). The young man sends some of his face paint but refuses the assignation. The wife puts on the face paint and to her husband accuses the young man falsely: "he just put the red-paint on my face and he lie with yonder" (Columbia p. 329). Boas misses out the accusation of sexual transgression, so when the chief becomes angry, it is, in Boas's narrative, only over face paint!

Boas footnotes the wife's speech in Tate's Tsimshian at the bottom of the page. This is an old device of Boas's and probably has honourable antecedents in nineteenth century ethnology. "Boas' Puritanism," writes Melville Jacobs (1959:123), "never stood in the way of getting dictations printed, even if, as in his earlier text volumes, he had to disguise a translation by putting it into Latin." I don't suppose James Teit himself would have cared a damn, but when Boas edited Teit's *Traditions of the Thompson River Indians of*

British Columbia (1898), all the spicey bits were put into Latin in the notes, where only theology students would be able to read them. It later dawned on him that the ideal languages for the purpose of obfuscation were the native languages themselves, since nobody at all could read them. Hence this footnote in Tsimshian (1916:217) just to avoid the phrase "lie with" in the English narrative.

Tate's Tsimshian word for "lie with" in this sexual connotation is "damkdut" (Columbia p. 329), which Boas gives in his footnote as "da'mxdut." If one looks the word up in the glossary (1916:972) it is there in its root form "damx" with a page reference to this footnote, but with no definition given, only a question mark. How deep will Boas's obtuseness go? He knows what it means; Tate's English and the context make it quite clear. But he is willing to deliberately spoil the story for the sake of avoiding the notion of sex—and he covers his tracks by feigning ignorance in a glossary entry.

In another story, Tate's sentence, "The man did not lie with his new wife" (Columbia p. 439) was left out by Boas (1916:75). We are not even allowed to think of sex that never happened. In this case we do not even get a footnote. In one place where Tate says a hunter touched a young woman's "belly" with his hand (Columbia p. 1036) Boas omits this "toned down" word from the narrative (1916:148): the hunter touched her, but where he touched her is, for scholarship's sake, put into a footnote in unreadable Tsimshian. On the Columbia manuscript p. 775 Tate uses the word "lust;" Boas substitutes the word "marry" (1916:161), with again the Tsimshian in the footnote. In another example, Tate says of a man and wife: "he lie with her there" (Columbia p. 1088). Boas cleans that up and says he "spoke to her" (1916:213) with the usual dollop of Tsimshian at the bottom of the page. Tate adds that "when they got through" the prince got up; that graphic bit is omitted by our arch-censor, with another dollop. It's funny really, because anyone who didn't know better might think that these footnotes were somehow acts of meticulous scholarship instead of a feeble excuse for suppressing any of Tate's candidness in sexual matters.

A final example shows how Boas's squeamishness not only blunts the edge of some of the story episodes but interferes with what one might call hard core ethnographic knowledge, the ritual for successful bear hunting. Tate explains the procedure in a sort of aside in the midst of a version of "The Girl Who Married the Bear" (Columbia pp. 734-35):

> ...twenty days lied down by himself alone, and he use one ceder bark mats, and he bath in two days at ten bath in each day's soon after each bath, he went to his wife or if he has no wife he will go to any woman he please, and lied down with her, soon after two days bath and lied with the woman, he took away the mats, and put it aside and took the new mats for the other twenty days. They use this custom when they wanted to succeed...

Boas omits from his printing of the story (1916:280) any mention of the sexual part of the ritual, again relegating it to a Tsimshian footnote. Thus, we are left with the impression that Tsimshian hunters are great ones for purification of sensuality before a hunt— or we would be if Boas had not later dealt with this in his "Description of the Tsimshian" section under the subheading "Religious and magical Practices." Here we get to the nub of Boas's egocentric predicament. What, I take it, Tate is saying is that there is a twenty day abstinence followed by two days of ten baths a day, each bath followed by a sexual encounter on the mat. Boas apparently could not take in the enormity of all that sexual activity in two days. In a strangely diminished intellectual state, his mind gave him a reading of Tate's passage where the hunter, during this twenty days of being alone, bathes and sleeps with a woman every other day. He gets into a terrible muddle (1916:449):

The bear hunter must live by himself and fast for
twenty days. During this time he must take a bath every
second day. After every bath he must lie with his wife,
or, if he has no wife, with some other woman. Then he
must put away the mat on which he has been sleeping
and use a new mat. During the whole period he must
keep away from his wife.

Boas adds: "The bear taboos are very complicated." No, Boas,
not true; only if you totally misread your source because of some
abaissement du niveau mental.

Though his deep disturbance shows through in the tangled
knots of explication, note that in this case Boas is willing to
mention coitus when he thinks it is required of him by the exaction
of science. His sanctimoniousness will not usually, however, allow
it into Tate's stories, neither as a motivation for revenge nor as a
mere chuckle. If Tate tones sexuality down, Boas obliterates it.
Who but Boas himself is preventing us from having, as he put it in
his 28 March 1907 letter, "a truthful picture of what the people
were"? One could add many more examples of censorship to those
given above. Each is of small consequence in itself (the reader can
usually get the point in spite of Boas), but they add up. I would say
that these little acts of cowardice, in toto, constitute a major
hypocrisy in the annals of anthropology.

Chapter Three

We have considered the "Christian influences" Boas spoke of (1916:31) in their censorship function; of equal importance is to take up the theological question of whether or not Tate's Christianity affected his story-telling in doctrinal ways. He wrote to Boas that he had deliberately curtailed the Raven cycle because it contained "very bad things," explaining that "we are a live in the christian life" (letter of 7 February 1907, previously quoted). One of the few things we know for sure about Henry Tate is that he participated in the Native evangelical branch of Rev. Thomas Crosby's mission (see Introduction). How does Tate's early Christian excitement affect the stories?

Again, we have to reckon with the transmission process, the "translation" from Tate's English to Boasian English. Science demands that Boas not interfere, but he is in a quandry. "Christian influences are evidently very strong among all tribes of northern British Columbia" (1916:31), but if they are too strong he patently lacks authentic texts. "At the time when I received these tales," Boas declares (1916:31), "I called his attention at once to the necessity of keeping strictly to the form in which the traditions are told by the Tsimshian." And did Tate get the message? Yes, according to Boas: "by far the greater part of the tales bear internal evidence of being a faithful record of the form in which the traditions are transmitted among the people" (1916:31). But here Boas is playing his cards very close to his chest. The tales "bear internal evidence of being a faithful record?" This diffident assertion makes us wonder if Boas doesn't know something we don't know.

We can begin our examination of this question with Tate's formal cosmology, the etiological "Sun and Moon" (1916 #8), which exists in a Tate manuscript located at the Smithsonian Institution Anthropological Archives. It begins at p. 195 in the Columbia sequence of numbering:

> It was about in the early days of before the Creation.
> There was no human being was livining on earth or any
> other places, but the lord in heaven was live there. And
> there was no light in heaven at that time but heaven
> was with form and void, and darkness was in heaven.
> And the Lord of heaven has two sons and one
> daughter...

Here is a man who knows his Genesis 1:2, even if he carelessly writes "with form and void" for "without form and void." In *Tsimshian Mythology* Boas's version mutes the Biblical echoes (1916:113):

> It was in the beginning, before anything that lives in
> our world was created. There was only the chief in
> heaven. There was no light in heaven. There were only
> emptiness and darkness.
> The chief had two sons and one daughter...

Tate's "lord in heaven" becomes "chief in heaven;" and the second time his "Lord of heaven" becomes merely "chief." Tate's "with [out] form and void" is stripped of its pointed allusiveness and becomes a secular "emptiness." This is really skimmed milk. A few other comparisons are given below:

Tate (Smithsonian)	Boas (1916)
deep darkness that covered them often (p. 196)	darkness was continuing all the time (p. 113)
we are so pleased to see they son give us light to lighten us (p. 198)	We are glad because your child has given us light (p. 113)
and all the multitude heaven make a great joy (p. 200)	and the whole crowd was full of joy (p. 114)
will brought good things to the whole world fruitful- ness and fatness (p. 210)	the duty to make all good things, such as fruit, appear on the earth (p. 116)

Boas is positively de-pentateuching Tate's vocabulary.[19] The result is to make Tate appear more authentic, more faithful to what Boas considered "the form in which the traditions are transmitted among the people" (1916:31).

Rather than worrying about authenticity, however, we might be more interested in how Tate's mix of cultures produces a viable story in its own right. It seems to me that Tate is very much his own man in this child's creation myth. As Boas says in his notes, "The essential element of the story is the transformation of two persons into Sun and Moon—an idea that seems to be foreign to other parts of the North Pacific coast" (1916:727). Or to put it more plainly, this is a unique story. It is a complete alternative to the widespread creation myth that Raven stole the sun and brought light to the world. How did the sun really come into being? One of two teenage brothers made a pitch mask, ignited it and ran across the sky before it burnt out. He was at first a bit quick, so his sister regulated things by holding him in the middle of his journey. That's why the sun stops briefly at midday. These are answers to a child's questions. They have the logic of the nursery. The other brother becomes the moon. The sister gets drenched in the western sea and returns to shake out her garments before the fire. Where did fog come from you ask? A natural question for anyone living on the shores of Hecate Strait. Tate has the answer, and I am quite prepared to believe that he remembered this just-so story from his childhood days or even made it up for his own children. Somebody did. If it wasn't somebody like Tate, it was Tate. Those striking allusions to Genesis, I'll wager, did not come from an oral rendering, but were an author's attempt to give weightiness to a pleasantry, to sustain him in the composition of a parable.

"Sun and Moon" actually contains patches of exposition, where Tate is simply explaining things like: "they have four season through year round. Spring, Summer, and Fall and Winter" (Smithsonian p. 207). It's a nice mixture of myth and quasi-science: when the sun sleeps, "the sparking forth from his mouth so it make the stars in the night, and the moon gets her light from the shining face of the sun while he was slept for he wearisome and his sun beamys out through smoke stark" (p. 208). Celestial snoring combined with something almost like the modern theory of the moon's light as a reflection of that of the sun. The precise nature of this cultural mix should be allowed to be seen. It too often in Boas's version is not. A further example would be in the naming of the months: "Between November and December" is, in the *Tsimshian Mythology* list (1916:115), "Taboo Month," which would be Dundas's conventional rendering of Tate's Tsimshian word "Hawulthk" (Smithsonian p. 206).[20] But in the manuscript we see, surprisingly, Tate referring to this Native division of the year as "name Nazarite." I do not think he means Christmas; December 25th would fall within the next division, "Between December and January." I believe Tate means to indicate that the Tsimshian have a holy month somewhat equivalent in its abstinence and spiritual power to the vow of a Nazarite in Numbers 6:1-21, where there are intricate rules of behavior and "all the days of his separation he is holy unto the Lord." Boas's methodology has meant that this interesting spanning of cultures has become lost.

There are further examples of where we learn from the original manuscripts how much Tate is living in two worlds and how he does not refrain from expressing this, though we do not see it in Boas's version. In the story "The Meeting of the Wild Animals" (1916 #2), Tate's phrase "herbs of the field" (Columbia p. 293) becomes "plants of the prairie" (1916:107), and "creeping thing that moves on the earth" (Columbia p. 295) becomes somewhat less Biblical as "those that creep on the ground" (1916:108). Strangely, it is to this story in particular that Boas pins the label "Christian influence," in a footnote not attached to King James phrases like those above (which, as we have seen, were anyway genetically modified), but solely in reference to the following (1916:106):

> ...it is in my mind to ask Him Who Made Us to give us
> more cold in winter... Let Him Who Made Us give to
> our earth severe cold... Let us ask Him Who Made Us
> to give to our earth cold winters...

The footnote says, "The term 'He Who Made Us' is presumably due to Christian influence. —F.B." This is very strange because Tate does not use these words at all. "He Who Made Us" is a fabrication of F.B.'s. Tate uses "our creation," "our Creation," and "Our creation" in those three passages above. One could understand an editorial change to "our Creator" but not to "He Who Made Us," unless one wanted to intentionally load the thing heavily towards the scriptural. It is as though Boas, having in his preface (1916:31) promised "Christian influences," wanted to show us a choice piece of evidence, and so pushed Tate's "Creator" up a notch to "He Who Made Us" in order to make the "Christian influence" point indisputable. But he does not want "Christian influences" everywhere, for fear his readers will consider he is serving them acculturated mishmash. He conspicuously manufactures one instance to take all the heat and shoves from sight as best he can most of the other, more genuine manifestations.

The possibility of Christian influence becomes a major issue in the first section of Tate's version of the Raven cycle, the origin of

Raven as a Creator figure in himself. Boas was put out by what he got from Tate; it was different from what he had reason to expect. "A Mrs. Lawson, who was married in Victoria, and whom I saw there in 1886," Boas writes in a letter of 22 May 1905, "once told me the beginning of the Tkamshum story." Boas then proceeds to summarize for Tate the version he wrote up in German in *Indianische Sagen von der Nord-Pacifische Küste Amerikas* (1895), which begins:

> A chief's wife has a lover, and her husband killed her.
> He put the body on top of a tree, and there a child was
> born, who lived in the intestines of his mother. One
> day the children were playing in the woods, and the boy
> jumped down from the top of the tree and took their
> arrows. The boys told about this at home, and then the
> chief got his young men to catch the boy, whose skin
> was bright as light.

"I wish you would tell me," Boas continues in the 22 May 1905 letter, "if some of the Tsimshian families tell the story in this way, and what families tell it in your way." Tate took this as an insult. "I am so very sorry for you have not believe at my history of Tkamshim beginning," he writes in a letter of 6 July 1905. He knows the story Boas is talking about: "If you want sucking intestines or chieftainness pretend to maggots, I shall send it down to you." Meanwhile, he holds firm to the correctness of the Raven origin myth as he sent it.

The problem for Boas was that it was unique; he had no analogues for it. He no doubt suspected Tate of deliberately suppressing the unsavory adultery of the "proper" birth story and substituting a kind of resurrection theme of post-European vintage, for this is what Tate had sent him:[21]

> There was once a land was covered with thick
> darkness, all over the world.

And there was a town of myth people at the south end of Queen-Charlotte-Island whose name is Kerouart Island.

It was before human person was live.

There was a chief of myth people and chieftainess were living there which they had a son an only son their parents loved him most.

Therefore his father make a bed for his son above them, as a Prince sign of a great loving Prince to keep him away from danger.

So the boy father build his son's bed above them into his large house.

They washed him regularly, and he grow up to be a youth.

And when he was quite young, and soon he was got very sick.

Then the young man groaned for he was very sick, and not long enough that he was died.

Therefore his parents deeply sorrow and mourning over their loved one that was lost.

Then the chief sent and invite all his tribes.

At once all the myth people come in, and when they all entered the house of the chief, as soon as they were all in, then the chief said Cut the belly of my dead son and take out the intestines.

Therefore his attendants cut the belly of the chief's dead son and took out his intestines and they burned it behind the chief house.

And they place the corpse on his own bed which his father build for him.

The chief and chieftainess have their mourning song in every early morning under the corpse of his dead son, with his tribe come in and have lamentation with them.

They have done it day by day, as long as the young man was died.

Then on the next morning very early that the chieftainess got up first, and she look up to where her dead son layed.

Then she behold a bright young man was sating down to where the corpse was layed.

Therefore she woke her husband and she said to him,

Behold our loving son is alive again.

So the chief got up from his bed and he went at the foot of the long ladder that reached the top up to where the corpse was layed above them, and he ascending towards his son, and he (chief) said at once,

Is it you my loving son my pet is it you?

Therefore the bright young man had said yes it was I.

As soon as this bright young man says yes, then the chief and chieftainess has bursted into joy and gladness. Then all his tribe came in as they did before to comfort their chief and chieftainess.

As soon as they entered they were much surprising for the bright young man was sat up now, and he spoke to them people,

The heaven was much annoyed for your often wailing every days, so he sent me down to comfort your sorrow.

So all the chief's tribe or his people was bursted into a great joy on that day, for their prince was alive again.

And the parents of this young man love him than they was love him before.

Boas's inclination to see this opening as a result of Christian influences is indicated by his giving a capital letter to the pronoun for the deity in a sentence near the end of the passage: "Heaven was much annoyed by your constant wailing, so He sent me down to comfort your minds" (1916:58) Tate did not capitalize "he" but maybe Boas is not far off track here. There is no miracle like this in the old stories. Raven, in Tate's version, is nothing less than a soul refurbished in heaven and destined for remarkable deeds: a resurrected son.

But we do not hear of Christ having been disembowelled. Tate is interweaving a bit of Native folklore—or is it really an old custom? Tate refers to it as such in parenthetical remarks in the later "Story of the Ghost" (1916 #56): "The custom is in the olden people when the Princes or rich men or Chiefs or Princess or some of the Ladies or they dear to them they cut round the deads belly and take out their bowells, stomach, hearts, livers, lungs, and when them empty the bellys they put some red-ceder-bark aukum in it, and they keep the body for a long while" (Columbia p. 1797; Boas puts this in a footnote 1916:337). This ghost story of the haunted house sort has no analogues and strikes one as an original composition. I do not know what later scholars have to say on the disembowelling question, but Tate believed it was traditional knowledge and therefore used it in portraying an honored dead prince. It was also traditional knowledge that the raven has had no intestines since the day he was so ashamed to come home without food for his children that he cut out his own innards and pretended they were some prize kill (1916:96). Raven in this later episode does the deed out of vanity, but the whole shamanistic tradition involves the notion of reduction to a skeleton and a rebirth with supernatural strengths. So Tate is hitting a lot of buttons in his opening paragraphs of the Raven cycle.

The resurrected youth has an aura like a Christian halo, but there are gods of light in many cultures and heroes of luminous aspect, and so it is with the Tsimshian, where the very word for "prince" contains the concept of light. As Marjorie Myers Halpin explains in her authoritative unpublished dissertation *The Tsimshian Crest System* (1973), the prefix refers to "bright and silvery young salmon," with a logical association with "the irridescence of abalone pearl" commonly used in crest artifacts: the title implies that the sons of chiefs "are as young and promising of wealth and plenty as the young salmon on its way down the river to the sea."[22] In short, young princes shine. Tate extended this concept to allegorical dimensions in the birth (or rebirth) of Raven, mixing Christianity and Native tradition.

Assumed in the discussion above is that Tate was writing the first section of his Raven cycle as a creative act of some originality. This speculation would be resisted in certain quarters. Boas manages to subsume it under his "Type III" (1916:636):

> Notwithstanding the differences between the versions
> treated here as Type III, it is fairly clear that similar
> ideas underlie all of them. In the first form the child of
> a dead woman sucks dry her intestines, and has a skin
> shining like fire. In the last version the intestines are
> removed from the body, which dries up, and from
> which proceeds the shining boy.

There seems to me a great difference between a shining youth who has fed on his mother's entrails (and is actually called "Sucking Intestines") and someone whose own insides were removed on death as a symbolic bid for eternity and whose resurrection as a shining youth was, in a sense, achieved thereby.

More telling is the testimony of a contemporary of Tate's, who was actually his stated source for "The Further History of Txamsem" (1916 #38, see p. 105). Henry Pierce, in 1935, told William Beynon that "Tate's version of the birth of Txemsem is the Haida version."[23] No such prior Haida story is in the record, but later, much later, in 1954, Beynon obtained Tate's version from a Skidegate Haida, Solomon Wilson. In its published form the pertinent part reads as follows (Barbeau 1961:83):

> The chief and his wife had a young son who seemed
> quite clever and was much loved by his parents. The
> young boy took ill and died. The people grieved greatly,
> and the chief erected a burial pole (or grave box) upon
> which he put the coffin of his son. Here, every day he

and his wife would come to mourn. Once, when the chief and his wife had come to mourn, they saw what seemed a bright shining light issuing from the box containing the remains of their son. As they drew closer, behold, a young boy sat upright. "Look," the mother cried; "our son has been returned to us." Both were extremely happy, and at once the bright shining boy was brought down. He said, "Because of your continual weeping and mourning, the chief of the Heavens has not been able to rest. So he has sent me back to you." The chief and his wife were very happy, as were the whole tribe.

This is so close to Tate that one wonders if in fact it came from Tate. Solomon Wilson is known to us through David Ellis's publications as a fine informant,[24] and I am not suggesting he palmed this off on Beynon as a Haida story; but we do not know the circumstances in which it was told. Beynon may have asked him if he knew this version, and he may have told it knowing it was Tsimshian. When he provides the name of the shining youth (see footnote p. 83) he has only the Tsimshian name to offer.

Boas had no knowledge of a Haida version like Tate's; he had for the Haida (see "Type II," 1916:625) something entirely different. But the chief witness to contradict Henry Pierce and the Haida theory is Tate himself. "I will go by the history of my peoples," he wrote in the 6 July 1905 letter, when he thought Boas was challenging him on this matter. And this one time he names his sources: "I have with me a three very wises olden men Chief Neash-ya-ganait and then two others Gilashgilash, and also E. Maxwell. These three olden men they are full wisdom. The chief was knew the beginning of Tkamsh'im history right to the end. The people are not live before Tkamshim coming down of our earth, until Tkamshim made person out of elderberrie tree. So I believed that my people knows very the history of Tkamshim than any other Indian round about us" (AMNH). Why indeed would

Tate be giving some obscure Haida version when he had these three heavy-duty story-tellers on call. They would not be leading him astray. The chief who is mentioned by Tate would be Herbert Wallace, who later was Marius Barbeau's "best teacher."[25] Enoch Maxwell was used as an informant by William Beynon in 1915; and the third we will probably never know the identity of (because Boas never bothered to ask Tate who these informants were), but he is meant to be a big gun like the others.

But three names is overkill. We would much prefer Tate to have given one, then we would not have to ask embarrassing questions about the process by which Tate conflated three tellings into one to produce a seamless story. Two of them are known informants, and did not offer Tate's version to anyone else. If I guess that the third, Gilashgilash, was actually Henry Pierce himself, it raises the even more embarrassing question as to whether or not any of the three gave Tate the resurrection version of the birth of Raven. Note that in his letter Tate does not specifically defend the very first part of his story, but mentions only Raven coming down to earth and creating humans from the elderberry bush rather than from stone. Elderberry bush? That's traditional; we're not worried about that. It's the very first part: where did that come from?

I cannot take Tate's protestations at face value. I know that he did not rely on his named sources for a great deal of the Raven story. After the parts he mentions (Raven's descent to earth and the elderberry tree), much came from another source entirely, as will be revealed. So there is little reason to think that the very first pages, unique at the time as far as our evidence goes, are anything other than a wonderful mythologizing on Tate's part. If this is true, then we are in the presence of an amazing audacity. How dare he do such a thing, how dare he be original?

This is where his Christian faith might come in. Tate knows of a God's son who outshines all local deities. I believe it came to him to give some of that power and glory to Raven. He drew on the very essence of the Christian story. The first drama in medieval literature was a short sketch allowed into the parish churches encapsulating a moment of "reversal" going a considerable way beyond anything in Greek tragedy. The three Marys approach the tomb to mourn over the dead Christ; the living Christ stands before them and says, "Whom seekest thou?" Tate, I believe, took this moment as his own and gave his traditional culture-hero the same kind of renewal. Or, in its greatest simplicity, as Bishop Ridley succinctly had it in his grammar,[26] something undoubtedly worked over and over by Tate, where on page 58, as an example of a syntactical construction, we find the sentence: "He that was dead sat up."

Christianity, in addition, offers something lacking in many mythologies: the reward of ecstasy. Tate is enabled to bring to the earliest beginnings of his nation a communal ecstasy: "all the chief's tribe or his people was bursted into a great joy on that day, for their prince was alive again."

Chapter Four

When Boas received the first 112 pages of the Raven saga he wrote to Tate on 22 May 1905: "In reading over the Tkamsham story, which is very interesting, and also the last story, which you sent me, I noticed that often the words that you use in the English translation are just the same as the words which I used in my Nass River stories" (AMNH). Boas is being disingenuous here in speaking of "English translation" when he knows that, as he puts it in the very same letter, Tate is writing "the English first." What he is really talking about is plagiarism.

Even the "Elderberry Bush" story (1916 #1(3)), which Tate cited in his reply of 6 July 1905, when he said, "I don't want to go on by or as the Naas history" (AMNH), is one of many of the Raven episodes that draws on the Nass River *Tsimshian Texts* (1902), which was among the volumes that Boas had sent to Port Simpson with his first inquiry. The short fable ends (see 1916:62):

Boas (1902) p. 72	Tate (MS pp. 385-6)
For that reason the Indians do not live many years. Because the Elderberry Bush gave birth to her children first, man dies	For that reason the people do not live many years. Its because the Elderberry-bush gave birth to her children first men dies

quickly. If the Stone had first given her children, this would not be so. Thus say the Indians. That is the story of the Elderberry Bush's children. The Indians are much troubled because the Stone did not give birth to her children first, for this is the reason that men die quickly	quickly. Or if the stone had first given birth to her children, this would not be so. Thus our people say. That is the story of the Elderberry-bushs children. So the Indians are much troubled because the stone did not give birth to her children first, for this reason, The people dies soon, and the Elderberry-bush grow on their grave.

Tate's extra comment about the Elderberry growing on the graves is a nice touch and almost redeems the theft that is going on here. I am not saying that Tate did not have independent knowledge of this myth and others in question, but clearly he preferred to use an easy method of writing down what he knew, easier than composing it afresh, easier than getting it by dictation from one of his named sources.[27] Boas, in the back of *Tsimshian Mythology*, notes a difference between the Nass version and Tate's (i.e. "The Nass version is not connected with the Raven legend" 1916:663) but he does not mention the blatant similarities.

In the case of "Origin of Daylight" (1916 #1(2)) Boas does go so far as to say "The Nass versions are quite similar to the Tsimshian form of the tale" (1916:649) but he does not explain why. We have to do side-by-side comparisons to realize it is simply copying (see 1916:61):

Boas (1902) p. 12	Tate (MS p. 379)
Then the chief and chieftainess were very glad. They washed him regularly, and he began to grow up.	Then the chief and chieftainess were much glad. They washed him regularly, the boy began to grow up,

Now he was beginning to creep about, and the chief smoothed and cleaned the floor of his house. Now the child was strong. He began to cry all the time, "Hamaxa, hamaxa!"	Now he was beginning to creep about. Then they washed him often, and the chief smoothed and cleaned the floor of his house, Now the child was strong, and creeping around every day. He began to cry all the time, "Hama, hama..."

Tate's quotation marks (for "Hama") are in themselves a give-away. He never uses such things except when he takes them from a text he has in front of him.

The point is that the Nass version and Tate's are not "quite similar," as Boas states in his notes; they are practically identical, the one copied from the other. Boas knew this; after all, he was reading in Tate's manuscript exactly what he himself had penned three years before. But he did not divulge it. In a small percentage of the cases some mention is made of similarities, and in his preface Boas states that a "few" of the stories indicate Tate's "familiarity with my collection of tales from Nass River" (1916:31), but he conceals the manner and extent of the wholesale plagiarism. Tate had his reasons—and one excuse could be that Boas from the start had asked him to write "in the manner of my Nass River book" (letter of 23 June 1903). Whatever Tate's culpability, Boas's dishonesty here is very serious indeed. Comparative folklore of the kind Boas practiced requires that one is comparing independent texts. If two independent texts are similar then that may say something about diffusion of myth motifs. If the texts are not independent, no such conclusions may be drawn. *Tsimshian Mythology* has a three hundred page section titled "Comparative Study of *Tsimshian Mythology*," where this principle should apply; it must now be realized that Boas has undermined his results in those areas where he has given the false impression that Tate has supplied independent texts.

What Boas loses by his subterfuge is not only our trust in his data but also the opportunity to see what is valuable in what Tate is actually doing. Whatever horrendous borrowing is going on, it is always interesting to see at what point Tate ceases to copy and injects into the narrative something of his own. For example, in "Origin of Daylight," Tate follows *Tsimshian Texts* (1902) up to the breaking open of the box containing the daylight. Raven's motive is the same: to thwart the people who are fishing in the darkness. In the Nass version these fisherfolk are ghosts who can manage better in the dark and who scatter at daylight. Tate forfeits the logic of that revenge, bowing to the preemption of a local legend where the mockers are frogs and their retribution is as follows (Columbia p. 384):

> Great person broke the Mha. It broke, and it was
> daylight. And then the north winds blew hard with the
> daylight, harder and harder then all them fishing men,
> frogs driven away by the north winds. Then all them
> frogs who made fun with WiGiat drivened away down
> until they arrived on one of the large Island mountain,
> here is all the frogs trying to climb up the rock, yet they
> sticked to the rock by the Frozen of North winds. There
> are now on the rock. They became to a rock. Those
> fishers frogs name him Tkeamshim, now the world have
> daylight.

I like the juxtaposition of light coming into the world with the ribbet-ribbet of frogs plastered to the rockface by sleet and managing, before they solidified, to croak out the Tsimshian name for Raven. Nobody seems to know what that name means, but if you imagine yourself an about-to-be-frozen frog, you might have some sense of the bitterness of the curse. Raven's first act is genocidal, and shapes on an "Island mountain" (known to Tate if not to us) remind us of it. The eternal event is interpenetrated with the morphology of the vernacular landscape.

Quantity is of the essence. How much use did Tate make of the volumes—there is a second source of borrowing—that came from Boas? We will take it seriatim, using Boas's numbering and titles in *Tsimshian Mythology.*

(1) "Origin of Txamsem"

Unique case, discussed above.

(2) "Origin of Daylight"

After two and a half paragraphs (1916:60) Tate begins to copy from Boas 1902 pp. 11-16; at the end he turns to a local legend, as discussed above.

(3) "Stone and Elderberry Bush"

Tate begins independently, but ends using the wording of Boas 1902:72.

(4) "Origin of Fire"

Widespread tale; no specific borrowing to be noted.

(5) "Txamsem Uses the Sinews of the Tomtit"

No known source. This tale was an afterthought, written at the end of the first batch of 112 pages, and inserted silently by Boas at this point according to Tate's instructions. That Tate has this kind of sense of the order of episodes is important to know. Unfortunately there is no obvious hint of why it should intervene here and it interrupts an existing continuity; so we might reserve judgment on Tate's organizational skills. Boas, in any case, should have mentioned the circumstance.

(6) "Origin of Tides"

Widely disseminated myth; no specific source.

(7) "Giant Gambles with Gull"

(8) "Giant Obtains the Olachen"

For these two short episodes, Tate carefully follows the wording of 1902:27-30. Boas's commentary (1916:654) mentions "Tsimshian, Nass, and Newette versions," and states: "The end is the same in all the different versions." He knows full well that the Tsimshian (Tate's) and the Nass (1902) are not different versions in the true sense of the word.

(9) "Giant Learns How to Cook Olachen"

(10) "Giant and the Gulls"

These two sections constitute an essay on food preparation, followed by a summary of the Raven episodes so far which is so conspicuously an expository statement that Boas felt he could only include it if he labelled it "Note of the Recorder" (deliberately perpetuating the fiction that Tate had gathered the texts in the field).

(11) "Txamsem and the Steelhead Salmon"

Tate begins by saying that Giant (Wi-Giat) has had a name change. He is now called Tkamshim. Boas in his notes does not remark on the fact that the frogs have already named him such. If he had done so he would also have had to say that the only reason Tate has for the present name change is that he has now turned to a different section of *Tsimshian Texts* (1902) where another informant uses Txamsem not Wi-Giat.

Tate copies pp. 52-55 of this source, up to the consultation of excrements about how to cook salmon. He saves the remainder of this episode in the 1902:55-56 version for use later (1916:89-90). There is a certain economy in some of Tate's moves, an authorial accomplishment that Boas feels himself not in a position to tell us about.

(12) "Txamsem and Lagobola"

With some embellishment and rearrangement Tate has taken this story from Boas 1902:17-20. This is not slavish copying, for Tate is alert to a problem on p. 20 during the bow and arrow contest: "'No; I hit it,' said Txamsem. He was very happy while he was saying this, therefore he used the Tsimshian language." Tate knew that this reference to Tsimshian would be illogical in a text of a Tsimshian speaker. He comes to, "No I hit it said Tkamshim. He was very glad, while he was saying this"—and stops the sentence right there, then continues copying with the Tsimshian reference missed out.

Boas does not take up this interesting elision, but in his commentary (1916:721) he feels compelled to express a suspicion, a suspicion he knows is more than a suspicion. He first asserts that this episode "has been collected only on Nass and Skeena Rivers." Boas knows that the tale he collected on the Nass was not collected separately by Tate but was copied by Tate. It is therefore less than ingenuous when he proceeds in a scrupulous tone to say: "I am not certain that the two versions are quite independent. Mr. Tate's Tsimshian version is so similar to the Nass version, that I am under the impression that the printed form of the latter was known to him" (1916:721). Of course the printed form of the Nass story was known to Tate; Boas sent it and has seen—probably with some horror and chagrin—Tate copy from it continuously. How could he pretend that he was not certain? And what does he do with this uncertainty masquerading as scholarly suspicion? Nothing. He leaves it alone. He pretends it is not important.

(13) "Txamsem and the Crab"

Source unknown.

(14) "Origin of the Bullhead"

This short "just so" story explaining how the bullhead fish obtained its strange shape is taken almost verbatim from 1902:37-38; but the few lines which are entirely Tate's are quite charming on how to entice a bullhead from the water:

> Txamsem stood there and wept. He said to the Fish,
> "You look like my grandfather, who died a little while
> ago." He wiped the tears from his eyes, and said,
> "Come ashore! I want to talk to you a while."[28]

It's a nice touch and shows what Tate can do when he ad-libs.

(15) "Txamsem Frightens Away the Owners of a Whale"

Source unknown.

(16) "Txamsem Finds a Beautiful Blanket"

Boas's note says innocently: "This incident is apparently confined to the Tsimshian and Nass" (1916:722). He does not say that Tate presents the Nass story in much of the same wording as 1902:38-39.

(17) "Txamsem and his Slave"

(18) "Txamsem Kills his Slave"

Tate knows the first slave story, but in the case of the death of the slave he relies entirely on Boas 1902:40-41. For example,

Boas (1902)	Tate (MS p. 432)
Then they came to a deep canyon. He took the dried stem of a skunk-cabbage (?) and laid it across. He made a bridge. Then he himself went across, and after he had done so he called K'ixo'm (that was the name of his slave) to come across; but the slave was afraid to follow Txamsem.	Soon they came to a deep canyon. Tkamshim had took the dried stem of a skunk cabbage, and laid it across, to make a bridge. Then he himself went across first, and when he got over on the other side, he called Lthgum, (that was the name of his slave) to come across; but the slave was afraid to follow him.

Note the identical phrasing, including the semi-colon (not in Tate's usual repertoire of punctuation marks).

There is more to be said here. The question mark is placed after "skunk-cabbage" because in 1902 Boas was not sure what was meant by the word "hok^u" in line 12 of the Native language text (1902:40). Later he decided it was wild celery rather than skunk-cabbage. We know this from p. 691 of *Tsimshian Mythology*, in his note on the above passage: "The Nass River version is the same as the last [i.e. Tate's] except that a stalk of wild celery (*hok^u*) is placed across the canyon." This is rank sophistry. We know that the two versions are the same because Tate is copying, in this case taking over the word "skunk-cabbage." Tate is not paying any attention at all to "hok^u"—which he cannot read—and Boas's later discovery of the word's meaning does not by one iota create an exception to their sameness. Tate would have put down "wild celery" if the words had been there; but they weren't: "skunk-cabbage" was, and that's what we get. Boas's point about "hok^u" is pure hokum.

(19) "Fishermen Break Off Txamsem's Jaw"

In his notes Boas admits that "the Nass version is identical with the Tsimshian version. Mr. Tate has evidently taken the former as a model" (1916:684). At last, when Tate is copying practically word for word the whole story, we get something like a full acknowledgment from Boas. Strangely, however, the acknowledgment seems to make not the slightest bit of difference. The line is that "by far the greater part of the tales bear internal evidence of being a faithful record of the form in which the traditions are transmitted among the people" (1916:31). Nothing will be allowed to shake that premise. Boas has seemed to have had the power of personality to make the shakiness of his scaffolding invisible.

(20) "Txamsem and the Hunter"

No known source.

(21) "Txamsem and the Children"

This is from 1902:42-43 with seal blubber changed to whale blubber. Boas (1916:686) notes this one difference without raising an eyebrow about the overall sameness.

(22) "Txamsem and the Salmon Woman"

Boas (1902) does not have this story, but another volume from Boas that Tate had on his table does. This is *Kwakiutl Texts*, the first two hundred and seventy pages of which were issued as *Memoirs of the Museum of Natural History* vol. 4 (January 1902).[29] For the last paragraph of this story (1916:78-79) Tate seems to have turned to this volume by Franz Boas and George Hunt. Certainly he has for the next story.

(23) "Txamsem Makes War on the South Wind"

Boas has a footnote to this story (1916:79): "The form of the following story is influenced by the Kwakiutl tale printed in Boas and Hunt, Kwakiutl Texts (*Publications of the Jesup North Pacific Expedition*, vol. III, p. 350)." That about sums it up, except he could have said it is very close indeed.

He almost does in the notes (1916:660), where he actually says that the *Kwakiutl Texts* version "is identical with the Tsimshian," but then spoils it by adding, "probably because it served as a model for the latter." Probably? If it is identical, there can be no uncertainty at all. The phrase "served as a model" is designed to make it seem innocuous, so that this can still be included as a Tsimshian story, not a copied Kwakiutl one.

(24) "Txamsem Makes a Girl Sick and then Cures Her"

No known specific source.

Of the 112 pages of the first Raven batch sent by Tate 9 May 1905, 39 pages were drawn from *Tsimshian Texts* (1902), 14 pages were derived from *Kwakiutl Texts* (1902), and 59 pages are independent of any known source. In other words, about half the material was, to use an old-fashioned word, plagiarized. Plagiarism is, of course, a very recent crime, a creation of the literary world where originality is at a premium. The oral tradition was made up of innumerable acts of plagiarism; you were supposed to learn and sing other people's sagas and tell an old tale with accuracy. In doing what he did, Tate is following this old tradition. In the end there is only one Raven episode in *Tsimshian Texts* (1902) that Tate doesn't send to Boas, and he may simply have overlooked it in the effort to make sure Boas got everything that he had asked for: "I am willing to engage myself at present to take 1000 pages written in Zimshian with translations between the lines in the manner of my Nass River book" (Boas letter 23 June 1903). This could easily be taken as a request to have the Nass River stories written out again but in the Tsimshian dialect. Requesting the "whole story" of Raven on 22 December 1903, Boas said, "I should like very much to have that story from the very beginning to the end, in the proper order." The "proper order"—that implies the *Tsimshian Texts* version is unsatisfactory and needs to be rearranged and made more complete. In fact, there are three overlapping Raven sequences in *Tsimshian Texts* (1902), so Tate may have felt he was being asked to sort it out into a continuous narrative, in part an editorial job. This is precisely what Tate attempted to do, and it fit well into his notion of what a traditional tribal story teller might do to expand his repertoire. What role Chief Neash-ya-ganait, E. Maxwell and Gilashgilash actually played in all this is hardly likely to become known; presumably they gave him, in some kind of story-telling context, some or all of the stories not taken from printed sources. But Tate's own memory of stories and his ability to creatively improvise must also be reckoned with. Perhaps, in the end, it might be that the three mentioned are those who gave Tate general encouragement and approval. There is a need for a great deal of further sensitive scholarship in this area.

As we have seen, when Boas read over this first batch of the Raven material he experienced something of a shock. He could see what Tate had done and he wrote forthwith on 22 May 1905 to tell him to desist:

> I should like it much better to have the stories told in
> just the same way as they are told by your people. I do
> not suppose that the way in which I wrote them down
> is just the way in which the best story-tellers tell them;
> and, from what little I know about the way of talking of
> the Tsimshian, they would not use just the same
> expressions as the Fort Rupert people. I would therefore
> beg to ask you, in writing the following parts of the

story, to write your Tsimshian first, just as your old
people are in the habit of telling the stories, and then to
write the English between the lines, and not to follow
my example or that of George Hunt (AMNH).

Better late than never. With that direct appeal Tate should have got
into line. But he did not mend his ways, neither in the interlinear
business nor in the borrowing.

It was over eighteen months later before Tate could get down to
completing the Raven cycle. On 7 February 1907 he sent thirteen
stories, seventy-five pages (Columbia pp. 477-551). Again, upon
examination, it appears that over half the stories depended to a
greater or lesser degree on the two printed sources.

(25) "Txamsem Pretends to Build a Canoe"

No known source; no analogues listed.

(26) "Txamsem visits Chief Echo"

Here Tate has in front of him *Tsimshian Texts* (1902) but he
paraphrases using occasional borrowings, such words as "proudly"
and "astonished." Towards the end he strikes out on his own,
demonstrating increasing skills in writing.

(27) "Txamsem Kills Little Pitch"

There is a literary transition from the previous story in that Tate
has the wife of pitch try to cure Raven's ankle that had been hurt
in the house of Chief Echo. She does so, appropriately, by applying
pitch as a medicinal procedure. After doing away with Little Pitch
Raven callously goes back to the house expecting a good supper
from the wife, but all he finds is a green spruce tree with a drop of
pitch on one side. These beginning and ending subtleties are
apparently unique with Tate, but all the middle part is heavily
dependent on Boas 1902. In his notes to the story (1916:683-84)
Boas mentions the differences but not the similarities, which really
are blatant. We can even see it in Boas's *Tsimshian Mythology*
rewrite. When one considers that Boas actually penned both of the
passages below it is nothing short of amazing.

Tsimshian Mythology (Boas 1916:87)
When the sun rose, Little Pitch wanted to go home; but
TxamsEm said, "I enjoy fishing. Lie down there in the
bow of the canoe, and cover yourself with a mat." Little
Pitch lay down, and TxamsEm called him, "Little
Pitch!" — "Hey!" he replied. After a while TxamsEm
called him again, "Little Pitch!" — "Hey!" he answered
again with a loud voice.

Tsimshian Texts (Boas 1902: 59)
When the sun rose Little Pitch wanted to go ashore, but
Txa'msEm said, "I enjoy the fishing. Lie down in the
bow of the canoe and cover yourself with a mat." Little
Pitch did so. Then Txa'msEm said, "Little Pitch!"
"Heh!" he replied. After a while Txa'msEm called again,
"Little Pitch!" He answered again in a loud voice.

(28) "Txamsem Kills Grizzly Bear"

This story is the old chestnut where the trickster pretends to
mutilate his own body in order to get his victim to do the same and
expire. The part of the body in question is often the privates. Thus
Boas 1902 p. 56: "Txamsem pretended to cut off his penis and to
tie it on to his hook for bait." Tate follows this (Columbia p. 496):
"Tkamshim pretended to cut off his penis and to tie it onto his
wooden hook for bait." He then got a bit squeamish and crossed
out "penis" and interlined with carots the phrase "part of his
bodies"; and then to lay down the red herring as thickly as possible
he crossed out "bodies" and substituted "heel." Boas can see
through all this: although he misreads "heel" as "belly" (1916:88),
in his notes (1916:681) he has an explanatory parenthesis, "belly
(evidently his testicles)," which at least gets it into the right vicinity.

Again Boas innocently declares that the "Nass River version is
practically the same" (1916:681), as though the two versions were
independent.

(29) "Txamsem Kills Deer"

Tate's narrative style generates its own momentum in this short traditional story, but essentially it is, as Boas's note says, "practically identical" with 1902:63-4, just adding a bit from 1902:55 in the middle. Tate is expansive and appends cooking instructions for good measure.

(30) "Txamsem Imitates Chief Seal"

Although this "bungling host" story is very widespread, Tate relies heavily on 1902:46-48, as he does for the next two similar stories.

(31) "Txamsem Imitates Chief Kingfisher"

(32) "Txamsem Imitates the Thrush"

Tate changes the name of Raven's host from "Salmon-berry-bird" (1902:49) to "Ripe-berries-bird" (Columbia p. 511) but never uses Thrush, which is Boas's word.

(33) "Txamsem and Cormorant"

This classic Raven story is present in Boas 1902:43-44 in a very truncated form. Boas, in his note (1916:679), calls it "quite similar" to Tate's, but this is not so. Tate preferred to turn to *Kwakiutl Texts* (1902) and, except for the first few and the last few lines, comes as close to copying as one can imagine. Boas neglected to mention this.

The ending, though again there is a deterioration in the grammar when he is not using a source, is interesting. Tate does what Hunt in the Kwakiutl story didn't: he has a dramatist's sense that Raven should have his comeuppance and supplies it (1916:93).

(34) "Txamsem and the Wolves"

(35) "Txamsem and Chief Grouse"

(36) "Txamsem Returns to the Wolves"

What Boas separates into three stories was, it seems, intended by Tate as a continuous narrative. A widely spread mytheme about Raven's greed is framed within a Wolf story which is possibly of Tate's own making, certainly a local brew. It has no analogues, is almost plotless, and sustains itself on a great deal of repetition. What distinguishes it is the portrait of a very kindly Wolf Chief, who has pity on Raven even after all the deceits are revealed. But in the end Raven has to flee and the nature of his escape is strikingly localized (Columbia p. 548): "Txamshim paddle over to alaska on the floating log. He from out side, or above the works channel over to Cape-Fox, he is drifting with the tired." These are familiar coordinates for Port Simpson people. Work Channel is the nearby fiord off the estuary of the Nass. Cape Fox is a promontory of Alaska across Chatham Sound. Boas, apparently to diminish the nonmythological content, left out mention of Work Channel and for Alaska substituted "the north country" (1916:100). But the local import seems to be the whole point: Raven's journey pacified the water for all subsequent canoe crossings: "so the canoes not capsize in the stormy weather when they cross over there, we call Mouth of Nass River until now" (Columbia p. 548). Tate seems to me to be at his best speaking of what he knows.

(37) "Txamsem Invites the Monsters"

This is a short piece to bow Raven off stage. The poor grammar and spelling indicate Tate was definitely not using a published source. None of the analogues cited by Boas have Raven turning himself into stone. It is apparently Tate's original idea: "This is the special end." (Columbia p. 551—this final sentence left out by Boas).

Since at least half of the second batch of the Raven cycle is indebted to printed sources, it is clear that Tate saw nothing wrong in continuing to "borrow." He had told Boas in his letter of 6 July 1905 (previously quoted) that he did not need the Nass River texts nor George Hunt, but that does not mean that he did not find it convenient to use them. Tate was doing what any oral story-teller would do: present in his own order things he had picked up from wherever they could be found, and adding his own spin. He knew he did not fill the bill of a real tribal story-teller, so he hustled to make up for his inexperience by lifting what he found close at hand from others he might well have considered more accomplished than himself, including the Nass River Philip and Moses and the Fort Rupert George Hunt, especially when he could read them in English in books sent to him by his employer as a model. Far from being harmful, this procedure produced a good result, as readers of Tate's manuscript can see for themselves. Even in Boas's rescension, the Raven cycle reads well.

With Boas, however, it is a different matter. We have to judge his role by scholarly standards, his own. Several times he indicates that Tate must have been influenced by a printed version without revealing the full extent or significance of the borrowing. Many cases of copying, including the most flagrant (the Cormorant story taken from George Hunt), Boas did not mention at all. This is bad enough. But when he simply notes, as he does a couple of times in the second batch, and many times earlier, that the Nass River and Tate's versions are identical, without saying why they are identical, then he leaves the impression that Nass people and Tsimshian people tell stories in exactly the same way. The cover-up of Tate's copying leads to a false scientific fact. Boas should have used his undoubted analytic abilities to describe exactly what was going on. We have begun that analysis here, and I do not think Tate suffers by it.

Chapter Five

We must now focus on another circumstance which created transmission difficulties. Boas made specific requests to Tate for stories. This is considered something of a no-no in the profession. "A direct request for a story," says Viola Garfield in the study previously cited, "may elicit quite a different response from that arising from other circumstances... The methods of the field worker should certainly be described, or made clear in the form of presentation." Boas does not make it clear that he asked for specific stories. "A favored device," Garfield continues, "is to cite a tale heard from a neighbouring tribe to stimulate discussion and telling of the local version" (Garfield 1953:28). Boas doesn't have time to be circuitous, and asks point blank for stories heard from another Port Simpsonite.

In his very first letter to Tate of 13 May 1903 Boas solicited the Raven story in some detail: "Now I will tell you what I should like to have first. I wish you could write the whole story in Tsimshian of Tkamsum, who was in the habit of taking the shape of the Raven,—how he was born; how NugumHat flew up to heaven with his friend after he had eaten his mother's intestines, all the stories that follow" (AMNH). He says more, but we will take up the thread begun here which leads finally to the story called "Sucking Intestines" (1916 #29).

In several letters after this first one, Boas reminds Tate about the Raven cycle and, in the letter of 22 May 1905 previously referred to, Boas spells out the version he is interested in. He got it in 1886 from a Mrs Lawson, whom he considered reliable because she was "the daughter of a Fort Simpson chief.."[30] Boas summarizes it for Tate: "A chief's wife has a lover, and her husband killed her. He put the body on top of a tree, and there a child was born, who lived in the intestines of his mother." If this version is still told, he asks, "I wish you would write this form also down for me." Boas repeated his request on 19 December 1906: "Will you not please go on and let me have the rest of the Tkemsum story, and the story of Sucking Intestines (Namomhat)?" (letter at American Philosophical Society, APS). Welcoming seventy-five further pages of Raven's adventures on 28 March 1907, Boas reminded Tate: "You will recall that you promised also the story of Sucking-Intestines (Namomhat). I hope you will find time to write it to me, and let me know how it is related to the Tkamsum story." On 16 August 1907 Boas is determined to pry out of Tate the "proper" beginning of the Raven cycle: "when you wrote to me last, in the spring, you promised to send the rest of the Tkemsum story and also the story of Namomhat (Sucking-Intestines)" (APS).

For all this badgering what does Boas get? He gets exactly what he is asking for, the "authoritative" version. Tate turns to the opening page of *Tsimshian Texts* (1902), and starts copying. Not slavishly. In fact he seems very much in command. He knows the story, and can be expansive, almost loquacious, but he is not averse to letting the 1902 version lead him and supply him with a smattering of the best dialogue.

This is the text he had in front of him (1902:7-9):

1. There was a town in which a chief and chieftainess were living. The chieftainess had done something bad. She had a lover, but the chief did not know it. The young man loved the chieftainess very much. He often went to the place where she lived with the chief. Then

the chieftainess resolved, "I will pretend to die." She pretended to be very sick, because she wanted to marry that man. After a short time she pretended to die. Then all the people cried. Before she died the chieftainess said, "Make a large box in which to bury me when I am dead." The people made a box and put her into it. They put it on the branches of a tree in the woods. The chieftainess had a spoon, and a fish knife in her box. She pretended to be dead. For two nights the chief went into the woods, and sat right under the box in which the chieftainess was lying. Then he ceased to cry. Behold, there were maggots falling down from the bottom of the box. Then the chief thought, "She is full of maggots." But actually the chieftainess was scraping the spoon with her fish knife, and the scrapings looked just like maggots. In the evening her lover went into the woods. He climbed the tree and knocked on the box, saying, "Let me in, ghost!" He said so twice. Then the chieftainess replied, "Ha-ha! I pretend to make maggots out of myself in your behalf." Then she opened the cover of the box, and the man lay down with her. He did so every night. Then she came to be pregnant. The man always went up to her. The chief did not know it, but one man found it out. He told the chief. Then the chief's nephews kept watch and killed the man, and also killed the woman. Now she was really dead, and her body was putrefying. Then her child came out alive. It sucked the intestines of its mother, and therefore its name was Sucking-intestines. The child grew up in the box.

One day all the children went into the woods, shooting with bows and arrows at a target. They were not far from this tree when they were shooting. Then Sucking-intestines saw them. He went down and took their arrows. Thus the children lost them again and again.

And so on, leading into the journey to heaven, where Raven gets himself born again as the chief of heaven's son.

Tate makes a much better story of this opening, giving himself the freedom of having it a separate short story. It was the purpose of my book, *The Porcupine Hunter and Other Stories,* to enhance the dramatic and prosodic features of Tate's style. Having suffered too much the tedium of the way Native traditional narratives are customarily presented, I could do no less than completely break away from the ill-fitting paragraph structure, and try to shape the prose on the page so as to conform to a dignified feeling which seems to be at the center of Tate's sensibility. Dell Hymes, Dennis Tedlock and Barre Toelken have taught us a new respect for the performance implicit in even the old published narratives.[31] It is impossible to match their expertise and attain the rigor of their methodology. The arrangement of Tate's text below (from *The Porcupine Hunter* pp. 158-62) is an instinctive response to the way the story, in his hands, seems to move.

The History of sucked the Intestine

There was a great town at Metlakahtla
   the village of Gishbakloush
      call Red bear Village
         in which a great chief and chieftainess
           and also the chief's nephew
             were living.

The young man
   fell in lover
      to the chieftainess
         which she love him most,
           but the chief
             did not know it.

The young man often
    went in to her
        and lied down with her
            while the chief was away.
        Then she became
            to be pregnant.

Then the chieftainess resolved
    I will pretend to die
        on your behalf
            so they all agreed.

So on the next day the chieftainess pretended to be very
sick, because she love the young man better than her
husband and she wanted to marry that young man. Not
many days since her sickness she said to her old husband,

        When I die you might bury me in a large
        box. Do not burn my body. Just put my
        horn spoon in my coffin, and my marten's
        garment and also my fish knife.

After a short time
    she pretended to die.
        Then all the chief's tribe gather
            and cried for her.

So the people make a large box to bury her. They put her
into it, with two marten blankets and one sea-otter
garment, also many dozen goodly horn spoon, with fish
knife, and they put it on the tree at the little Island at the
front of the Village.

                      Now she pretended

to be dead.

After two nights
    that the chief
        went over the little Island,
           and sat
                right under the coffin
                    into which the chieftainess
                        was lying.

His weeping.

Then while he was there
    he beheld grubs
        falling down
            from the chieftainess' coffin.
              Then the chief thought
                she is full of grubs
                    so he make him
                        wept bitterly.
(But the chieftainess actually, scraping the spoon horn with her fish knife into the coffin, so the scraping the horn spoon lookeds just like as maggots.)

And since the chieftainess was in her coffin, that the young man went into her every night, in her coffin, while the village people was all slept. He went over the little Island, and he climbed on the tree and kicked the cover of the coffin saying,
            Let me in to you, ghost.
Then the chieftainess was laugh in her coffin bed,
                Ha ha-ay
                in your behalf
                I pretended
                to make grubs
                myself.
So she opened her coffin cover and the man went in and lay down with her. The young man always went up to her

every night. But the great chief did not know it. He still weeping, no one could comfort him.

The other night some another young people went over that little island where the chieftainess layed. They soon sats with his sweetheart under the chieftainess' coffin. They behold a young man coming over to where they was.
They knew it was the chief's nephew.
He climbed up to where the chieftainess' coffin, he kick the coffin cover, he says, Let me in to you, ghost. Then they heard the chieftainess was laughing in her coffin. They heard her replied, Ha ha-ay, I pretended to make maggots of myself in your behalf. They saw the young man went into her coffin,
> and this young couple
> heard that was played
> in the coffin.
> Then before the day light
> that the nephew of the chief
> come out from the coffin.

Then they told it to the chief.

So the chief send over his two attendants to kept watch the chieftainess' coffin, and he commanded them, If it is sure, throw down the coffin. Therefore these two attendants went over. They watch the coffin, and while village people was sleep they behold a man coming over. They knew it was the chief's nephew. He climbed up the tree to where chieftainess layed. Soon as he reached the top the coffin, he kicked the coffin cover, saying,
> Let me in to you, ghost.
They heard chieftainess laughing. She replied,
> Ha ha-ay
> I pretended

to make maggots
out of your behalf.

These attendants heard
there was played
in the coffin
and at midnight
they heard
their was ceased.

We might interrupt the story to note that Tate likes the coffin scene so much that he finds a way to do it twice. One might also note that both times, instead of the euphemistic word "playing," Boas substituted a supra-euphemism, "talking" (1916:215-16). Through the "playing"—the self-absorption of the two of them and the delay in discovery—Tate quite skilfully builds up suspense. But he is coming to the end of the episode and has to make a decision about the ending.

These attendants knew their was slept, therefore they climbed on the tree and they threw down the large coffin.
The chieftainess was bursted
and the chiefs nephew also was killed.

And when these men come down
they saw a baby boy
was among the intestines
of his mother.

They went into the chief's house. They told him it was true. They told him also that the child was alive. Then the chief order them to bring the child to him, so they brought the child to him.

It sucked the intestines of its mother.
Therefore the child name was "Sucking-Intestines."

This is where the story could end. He has done his job. He is not going to follow the Nass 1902 version and take Namomhat up to heaven. He is on record that this story is not part of the Raven myth. If he does not stop here, then he has to come up with an ending that will make it ring true as an independent story. I said in my article (Maud 1989:161) that Tate's solution was a symbolic outcome worthy of Nathaniel Hawthorne. That was not, I hope it was clear, in the highest category of praise, but there is a rightness to this ending, a superficial rightness leading to pathos. I still consider the comparison with Hawthorne valid.

Then the chief take one of good female slave to be
his nurse.

The child grew up in chiefs house, and the chief love the little boy most. And when the boy was able to walk, he went over often to that little Island to get Spruce chewing-gum, for he likes chewing-gum best at the same Spruce where his mother's coffin was on while she pretended to make maggots out of herself. And the chief took him over and burnt him some pitch with fire to let the child chewing. With some of his slaves they did it so many time.

The boy walked over
    alone to that Island
        and get gum   out of the same Spruce
      to his mother's grave.

His mind was set
    on the little Island

to where his born.

He played around the island   almost every day
so the slaves took him over there.

He became a beautiful young boy. Now the chief
love him more every day. Therefore on the next day that
the young boy said to his father (the chief), Let us go
over to that little Island and burnt off the pitch with
fire. So the chief went with him, and some of his slaves.
Then the chief order his male slave to burnt off the
pitch. So they did. They burnt pitch. Then the chief sat
near the Spruce with the boy stood at the front of him.

> Then the flamed of the fire
> > like a tongue
> > > took the boy
> > from the chiefs bosom.
> And the boy was burnt to dead,
> > and the chief was mourned again.
> > > For the fire swallowed up the boy.

It is just not fair that the boy should die this way. He is possessed
by a spirit power not translatable into social significance. The story
is convoluted in on itself. The spruce gum is a form of chewing his
mother, is it not? I do not know of any commentator who has
taken up the possible depth of meaning in the hero's sucking the
intestines of his mother and then turning to the resin of the tree in
which she held the trysts that produced his birth. Here is a
putrefaction and metamorphosis to match the symbolism of the
Samson story where honey is made by bees swarming in the carcase
of a lion he killed. Raven is weaned on offal—that much is clear
when this "Sucking-Intestines" episode is attached to the Raven
cycle. His disreputable carrion crow nature has that origin. But
Tate's "Sucking-Intestines" becomes a nice boy chewing gum, or so

it is made to seem. And his death is tragic to the feeling chief. Is it a mother's rage that lashes out and takes the child from his adoptive father? Or is it the mother's ardent love that brings him to her in a tongue of flame? It is this kind of offered alternative that Hawthorne often tantalizes his readers with. I do not think that, in the end, it is very kind to leave the reader in the dark, but ambiguity of this order is not uninteresting.

Tate adds two explanatory sentences to the story:

> Now this is the end of "Sucking-Intestines." Now we call this little Island "She-Pretended-To-Make-Grubs."

Did Tate have a specific place in mind? His Tsimshian name for the island, Lakshishtaksha'andh, is not known, but it was probably not fictional. Maybe this is a locally-told story after all, a place-name story, nothing "creative" about it. I still am convinced, however, that Tate created the ending of the story to fit his notion of a proper denouement, and then added the place-name like many a novelist to make the fiction seem more real. It would be nice to know for sure the answer to some of these doubts. Boas wrote many times nagging Tate for this story, but didn't write to ask him anything about it when it turned out to have anomolous and intriguing features.

Chapter Six

In the only challenging review of *Tsimshian Mythology*, Marius Barbeau picked out the epic story titled "Gauo" to illustrate his suspicion that Tate is not totally reliable (Barbeau 1917:562):

> In writing down from memory a lengthy and complex tradition, Tate is liable to have forgotten or slightly altered many accessories or even supplied some out of his own stock of familiar notions. We have noticed, at one or two places, that his information as to the identity of crests spoken of in myths differs from that which we recorded with expert informants. Tate, moreover, relates these stories as if he were speaking to a stranger. For instance, he says (p. 389): "...In olden times, people cleared their land with stone axes..." Such details on culture perspectives do not enter into the undisturbed Indian narratives. Interpolation of a more important nature is to be found in the myth of Gao''a'. After having given the full text of the myth, which, in four other versions in our possession ends without explaining its connection with present-day social units, he goes on, with more than four pages of explanation on the origin of the Tsimshian (and Tlingit) phratries,

clans, crests, tribes, relationship and so forth. Interesting as may be a native's attitude towards the problems of ethnology, it is usually far from being a criterion of truth. It should, besides, reveal itself under its own colors. Tate's views here are not altogether acceptable and as they are supposedly part of a traditional text they are decidedly misleading.

This is strong criticism. There are several contentions here that need to be evaluated, but it all adds up to one big black eye for Boas.

"Gauo" is a thoroughgoing revenge tragedy involving two villages, one on each side of the Nass river. A leading figure in our village (if we identify with the Gispawadweda, the Killer Whale clan that Tate was adopted into) is Gauo, a wealthy chieftainess, who has four sons and a daughter. The eldest son was not having the luck of his brothers on their two month hunting trip and, in trying to unblock a beaver dam, he was struck by timber and killed. Bad luck like this means that one's wife has been unfaithful; it seems to be an infallible assumption in these stories, and so it is here. The youngest brother takes it on himself to investigate and proceeds to murder the interloper in a passage of memorable story-telling by Tate (1912:195-96):

> Then he staid in the woods, waiting for the night to come. When it was night and it was dark, he went slowly down to a place near the house. When he came to the rear of the house, he heard in his ear secret talking at the place where the wife of his brother lay, and they laughed and whispered. Then the young man knew that a person lay with his sister-in-law. He waited until they slept. When it was midnight, they slept. Then he entered very slowly. He went to his mother. Then he wakened his mother, and the man asked his mother, "Does not a man lie near the wife of my

brother?" Then his mother replied, "I don't know."

Then the young man told his mother all that had
happened. He said to his mother, "Don't cry! I shall kill
the man who lies with my sister-in-law." Then the
chieftainess cried very much. She cried aloud
aɫg·a'ɫg·aɫg·aɫ. Then her daughter-in-law asked her why
she was crying and she said that she had dreamed that
her son was dead. Then he stopped his mother.

He lighted a torch of pitch-wood and slowly went
towards the place where his sister-in-law lay. Then he
took a large knife in his right hand and the torch in his
left. He came to the place where his sister-in-law lay.
When he came near, he saw the arm of the woman as a
pillow of the youth who lay with her. Then the young
man put down the torch. He took the man by the
forehead and cut off his neck with his knife. Then he
went out with the head,—the head which was covered
with abalone ear-ornaments and killer-whale teeth, very
expensive ones. That man whose head he had cut off
was the son of the master of the other village.

Then the woman took the body of the young man who
had been with her, and buried it under the place where
she had lain.

When Gauo says, "I don't know," the story is evoking that direst of
dramatic tension, that between what a character knows and what
she won't allow herself to know. If this moment reminds us of the
fragment that Dell Hymes and others have spent much time on,
"Seal and her Younger Brother Lived There," it should, for they are
similar episodes in the same overall revenge story and have the
same layered intimacy (Hymes 1981:274). Confined space always
leads to the agonistic; the northwest coastal long houses must have

had as much repression and intrigue per square foot as any casbah. The unfaithful daughter-in-law buries the headless body within the house at the sexual center of her widowhood: who was averting their gaze from that intimacy and treachery?

The murder is discovered by the other village, which wipes out our side except for Gauo and her daughter, who had hidden in a cave. In some way the central core of the story is the choice of a marriage partner for the daughter, a catalogue of fowls and fauna. The plot stands still until a suitor from the sky gains her hand, and their sons reinhabit the village and achieve ascendancy over their enemies with the aid of a supernatural box that, when opened, induces a local earthquake fissure. We win. (At least, in Tate's version.)

This is a rushed summary because the point at issue is not the story proper but Tate's appendices. Barbeau has had this story from four other people, but they didn't start giving a lecture "on the origin of the Tsimshian (and Tlingit) phratries, clans, crests, tribes, relationship and so forth" (Barbeau 1917:562) No Tsimshian would dream of pontificating in this way to an Native audience: Tate sounds like an ethnologist. What Barbeau does not know is that this lapse of authenticity is entirely due to Tate's responding to a specific detailed request of Boas's. His very first instructions (letter of 13 May 1903 AMNH) included the following paragraph:

> Then there is another thing which is just as important, and that is the history of the very beginning of the Ganhada Gispawaduwada Lakskiek Lakkebo, who were the first ancestors of these families, and how they gradually spread and formed the different families in the different villages, with whatever tales belong to the histories of these families.

So what can Tate do but end his Gauo tale with the victory of the four sons of Gauo's daughter, and then without pause apply himself to answering Boas's request (1912:217-19):

87

Then they went about among all the villages to make
the clans in every village. If the people of a village
refused, they made war again. Then they went from one
village to another, and they tried again to make the
clans among them. When they agreed, they went to
them. Then they did not fight.

Then they went to the Tlingit everywhere and came
back. Then they went southward along the coast to
force all the villages of the Tsimshian to make the clans.
Thus began the four clans: first the G·ispawutwa´da,
then they are together like one company,—Bear, Killer-
Whale, Moon, Star, Rainbow, and many others; and
next there are the Eagle and they are also like one
company,—Eagle, Beaver, Halibut, and also others.
Raven and Frog, and Sea-Lion and Starfish and others
are the crests of the Ganha´da; Wolf and Crane and
others are the crests of the Wolves.

And so it goes for a further few pages. This is where, if it was ever
part of the story, the children would have gone to sleep. But as
William Beynon wrote in 1933 in his notes reviewing this passage,
"This really does not form part of the Gao'a myth, as I have it
recorded"[32]—the point we have already seen enunciated in
Barbeau 1917:562. And we reiterate: Tate knew quite well what he
had done and why. The text as printed (1912:225) makes this clear
in its final comment: "This is the end of the story of Gauo and part
of the customs of the Tsimshian." Two things. It should have been
obvious to Barbeau that at a certain point the narrative had moved
across a genre line to become exposition. Of course, if Boas, as editor,
had ended the story where the story properly ends and reserved the
rest for the ethnographic description section of *Tsimshian Mythology*,
then there would have been no confusion at all.

Barbeau's criticism goes further, however, to the heart of Boas's
scholarly method: "The foundation of Dr. Boas's conclusions as to

the origin of the Gispuwudwada, the Wolf, the Raven and the Eagle phratries seems to illustrate our point as to how misleading is secondary and incomplete evidence, when too much reliance is placed upon it" (1917:553). A knowledgeable scholar would have known that "only three or four royal households are considered as the actual descendants of the four mythic sons of Gaoa, and, as such, enjoy the use of their crests" (1917:554). Tate had the four sons going everywhere and laying the law down universally. All he was doing, I believe, was extrapolating on Boas's original formulation when he wanted to know "who were the first ancestors of these families, and how they gradually spread and formed the different families in the different villages" (letter 13 May 1903 previously quoted). Boas meant how did they, the families, spread, but Tate takes it as how did they, the first ancestors, spread the crests, and tacks on to "Gauo" this spreading as an act of cultural conquest.

In his formal "Description of the Tsimshian"—since it is not his practice to express doubt about his informants—Boas solemnly puts it: "Whatever the further descent may have been, the crests were first given by the Sky chief to his son's children" (1916:414). And again: "a rather obscure statement in the Gauo story has it that the children of the Sky Being, who were sent back to earth with their crests, made war on all the tribes, and compelled them to adopt the clan system" (1916:411)—although, in calling this "a rather obscure statement," he is vaguely hinting that things may have got on the wrong track somehow. We know how. Tate wanted to please, and took his cue from Boas's specific request. Unfortunately, he read the cue wrong, causing a problem that later students of Tsimshian mythic history have to try to sort out.

Once we know the full story, Tate's role is understandable. As it is presented in *Tsimshian Mythology*, Tate is left vulnerable as a target, and Marius Barbeau, in his over-zealousness, can say in his review such things as "scantiness of his data" and "evident lack of insight evinced by Tate" (1917:557). And further: "Although Dr. Boas's description of the Tsimshian is convincing and probably accurate on the whole, we have found it imperfect in the only field that we have tested—that of social organization—owing to the fact that the text material furnished to him by Tate was one-sided and very incomplete" (1917:552). Barbeau's real beef, I should think, is not that Tate is limited in what he has to offer, which is to be expected of any single person, but that Boas does not, on principle, accept that Tate is such. The individual is the tribe: this is the erroneous notion behind the annoying assertiveness of Boas's exposition.

Barbeau had special cause to be annoyed at Boas's presentation of the social organization of the Tsimshian on Tate's say-so alone, because he did in fact write out for Boas his own tentative conclusions from his work with Beynon. While still in Port Simpson he received from Boas page proofs of *Tsimshian Mythology* and inundated Boas with material, as catalogued in John Freeman's *A Guide to Manuscripts Relating to the American Indian in the Library of the American Philosophical Society* (Philadelphia 1966) p. 373, item 3768:

> BARBEAU, C. MARIUS. Social organization of the Gitzaxtet tribes [1915]. Typed D. and A.D. 30p.
>
> Revision of formal paper. Lists Gitzaxtet [Tsimshian] houses and crests; typed copy with annotations of Edward Sapir. Covering letter of Barbeau to Franz Boas, Feb. 1, 1915, in which Barbeau discusses phonetics, social organization, and crests; disagrees with some of the Tate material upon which Boas based his Tsimshian mythology.

There is also a letter of 14 February 1915 with detailed corrections of what Boas was proposing to put into *Tsimshian Mythology* on this question. Boas ignored all this material, except for a little linguistic help—as he put it in the preface, "I am indebted to Mr. C.M. Barbeau for the phonetic equivalents of some Tsimshian names used by Mr. Tate" (1916:32). Other help he spurned, thinking it best to stay entirely with his own informant, right or wrong. He thus laid himself open to the disdainful animus of Barbeau's review.

Barbeau's judgments are, as they stand, utterly devastating to Boas's imperious posture, and put Tate himself into ill repute. Boas should have defended Tate in a full-scale rebuttal of Barbeau. Even on as simple a matter as the scope and balance of Tate's corpus of stories, Boas could have refuted Barbeau's accusation that Tate did not collect enough crest stories. Boas lists them on 1916:411-412; they number nineteen, with certainly "The Feast of the Mountain Goats" and "Asdiwal" to be added and probably several others. This is twice as many as Barbeau is willing to grant Tate in his footnote 1917:553. This could have been forcefully mentioned.

Boas could also have pointed out that Tate, in mainly giving stories outside their crest validation function, was doing us all a favour. When a property-owner gets going on a narrative whose only purpose is to prove what a bigwig he is and how other family crests are insignificant in comparison with his own, good story-telling fades into vanity. Even if traditional themes and episodes are incorporated into the crest quest, they are subordinated to the need for aggregation, making sure that no bit of abalone shell is left out. Where Tate's stories get closest to the usual crest narratives, e.g. "The Drifting Log," or "The Water Being Who Married the Princess," an interminable tediousness sets in, the log drifts. Crest stories are boring to anyone not party to the one-upmanship of the potlatch game. Boas could have said, in reply to Barbeau's "I have more cresties than you," that crest stories are the pits and we should be glad that Tate didn't—if it's true he didn't—have as much access to that upper class world as Beynon. Boas could have come out fighting in defence of the recently deceased Tate. But he did not reply at all to Barbeau's review, and thus the irksome libels remain. Boas couldn't rise to it because it would have meant a complete reexamination of his own position.

Chapter Seven

This chapter discusses Boas as a literary critic. A literary critic, on the basis of much reading and analysis of texts, will try to say what ought to be valued and why. I have discovered only one occasion on which Boas expresses a preference for certain stories and says why. He puts his money on Henry Tate. But nowhere in *Tsimshian Mythology* does he say he enjoys Tate's stories; we have to wait until a late volume, *Kwakiutl Culture as Reflected in Mythology* (1935), to finally get a value judgment: "it may be said that in Kwakiutl stories dealing with human society the interest is mainly sustained by their specific interest in rank and privileges and that without this they are lacking in variety of subject matter and in skill in composition. The general human interest and the imaginative power exhibited by the Tsimshian is much greater" (1935:190). Boas finally comes clean: he prefers Tate's work to Hunt's. Since George Hunt had died in 1933, Boas cannot now hurt the feelings of his old friend.

Let us say from the start that Boas's judgment here is rather a safe one. The mass of Kwakiutl stories filtered through the mind and pen of George Hunt is quite possibly the most dreary literary production that the world has ever been presented with. Hunt has given native texts a reputation for monotone from which they may never recover. So it is not great praise to say that Tate is better than the worst. Nevertheless, it is comforting to hear it said: Tate has superior "general human interest" and "imaginative power."

Not only that, but Boas is willing to be specific: "the plots of the Tsimshian stories are more varied and more coherent than those of the Kwakiutl. A few examples will illustrate this" (1935:185). Boas proceeds to outline the plots of a couple of stories from each area. Better yet, one of these four plot summaries (and here we get to the nub) is followed by a sentence which qualifies as literary criticism: "Although the story consists of two independent parts each is well unified and based on situations that are appealing even outside the range of North West Coast culture" (1935:186).

This, for what it is worth, is the only literary judgment on a specific story in all of Boas's works.[33] He says (1) the story has unity—albeit in two parts. No, it's the two parts that have their own unity, and the story itself obviously therefore doesn't. If unity is a value, then surely Boas could pick out a story which is itself unified. There are scores of them. Anyway, (2) the story is praised because it can actually appeal to Europeans (I suppose that is what Boas means by "outside the range of North West Coast culture"). Both (1) and (2) are quite ethnocentric, and (2) contains a bit of a slur. What Boas perhaps meant to say is that the story contains universal appeal, as we expect a classic to do. We can only guess what he meant to say, for he offers no further word in elaboration. Boas's claim to be a discerning reader rests entirely on these two comments.

The best we can do is to turn to the story in question and test the timbre of Boas's insight against our own sense of the unity and appeal therein. I am all the more eager to use this particular story because it is the well-known "Asdiwal" story, used by Claude Lévi-Strauss for one of his famous flights of structuralist fancy.

1. The Story of Asdi-wā'l; or, The Meeting on the Ice.

Well, when a great famine reached [touched] the people of the Skeena, then a chieftainess was also among the

starving people, and a young woman who had married
a man of a town way up the river. Her mother, however,
was in her own village at Canyon. That town is way
down the river, that was when the great famine reached
[touched] the villages.

Then the husband of the chieftainess died, and the
husband of the young woman also died of starvation,
for the starvation in the villages was really great:
therefore many died.

Then one day the chieftainess talked to herself when
she was hungry: therefore she said, "I remember when I
used to meet my daughter." Then the young woman
also said, "I remember (think) when I meet my mother
when I go down the river, when I go near her, then I
shall eat food, then I shall have enough to eat."

(Well, the famine struck [the people] every year in the
winter, when it was very cold. It was that which cleared
off all the people: therefore they died.)

Therefore one day the chieftainess arose to go on the ice
to the young woman. On the same day the young
woman also arose to go also to her mother. Therefore
she also went on the ice.

Then they met between the two towns on the ice. They
were both very hungry, (she) and her daughter. There
was nothing to eat. Both were left (alone) by death,
(she) and her mother. Then they sat down and waited
and wept because of their husbands, who had died of
starvation.

When they had cried for some time, they stopped
wailing. Then they went ashore to make a camp at the

foot of a large tree. Then the young woman went about. Then she found one rotten hawberry. Then she gave to her mother one half of the rotten hawberry, and she herself ate (the other) half.

Then she made a small house of branches, and they began to drill fire to make a fire in a small house of branches, where they lay down. Before they lay down, they made a great fire to lie down warmly. Then they slept well. On one side of the fire the old woman, on her part, lay down with her back to the fire; and on (the other) side the little noble woman, on her part, lay down; they were with their backs towards the fire.

This is the beginning (1912:71, 73) of a story that is thirty-eight printed pages in all. We will have to resort to paraphrase and summary along the way; but not yet or we will lose the flavour and dynamics of the way the story-teller is putting it over. Boas's abstract of these opening paragraphs doesn't help (1935:185):

There is starvation in two villages. A mother lives in one, her daughter in the other. They start from their homes each hoping to find help in the other's village. They meet on the ice and deplore their situation.

Boas has relieved himself of many of the burdens literary critics take on themselves: he has announced that his only criteria will be variety and coherence of the plot, not the diction, characters, tempo, realism, symbolism, or anything else about a story. Consequently, he feels he has no need to concern us with quotations; summaries will do very well for his purposes.

This means we have to explore for ourselves the manifest literary values that inhere in the texture rather than in the broad strokes of the story. We cannot, for instance, let this opening of "Adsiwal" go by without noting the way in which the story-teller is getting into gear, finding his voice, repeating things (the background famine), just waiting, it seems, for his audience to quieten down and attend. Of all Tate's stories this one—his first one, by the way—seems closest to an actual oral recital. The first word "Well" certainly contributes to that effect (and who knows how many other *wells* were dropped in the transmission—we don't have Tate's manuscript to check up on it). I feel I hear a crusty old voice here, with the implied reproach: you people think you have it bad? You don't know anything about real privation. I feel the narrator's positive awe of the coincidence: that a mother and daughter should set off at exactly the same time and meet on the ice in the middle of the frozen Skeena river. "The Meeting on Ice" is made the co-title of the story even though it is only the first of many daunting events. I see him stretching his arms to indicate the distance to be traveled by the mother up river and the daughter down—or maybe using the length of the long house for maximum effect. There is no reason to suppose that story-tellers always sat. If there is nothing but one rotten hawberry to be found, can't that be shown in a facial expression, with the eyes focussed on the fingertips held before one's face? Then the dividing of it and the nibbling... There is so much going on here that a master entertainer can use. To sleep well on half a hawberry, it must be the fire that does it. You get your back as close as you can to the fire and curl up on yourself tightly. This whole first section has a marvellously confident air to it. A like-minded, loving mother and daughter, after terrible loss and hardship, say "That's enough," and take individual action. They leave the enclosure of their villages, they seek, they scavenge, they build a fire, they sleep well from the effort of having made a move. Boas fails to capture this positiveness in his summary: "They meet on the ice and deplore their situation." They deplored all right: they were bringing one to the other the news of the death of father and son-in-law. However, when they had cried for some time, says Tate's story, "they stopped wailing. Then they went ashore to make a camp" (1912:73).

I don't know if there is a Tsimshian proverb about the gods helping those who help themselves. If there is, it is hovering in the background of this tale, which continues (1912:73):

> When it was midnight, a man entered (and went) to the little noble woman. He went to her and lay down, and they lay down together. The old woman did not notice it. Early in the morning, the young man arose and went out. Then they, on their part, saw that their fire was about to be extinguished.
>
> Then the young noble woman arose again (and went) to get bark. When she went out, she heard the one sing whose name is Hats!Enā´s. (It is like a robin, but it is not he. When somebody hears Hats!Enā´s speak, he has good luck with whatever he wishes. That is the reason why the name of that bird is Hats!Enā´s ["Good Luck"]).

The story never tells us anything of the motives of the supernatural being, Good Luck, who sings like a bird and lays like a man who has been on the lookout for a damsel in distress. I wonder if this is one those situations mentioned by Boas that "are appealing even outside the range of North West Coast culture" (1935:186, quoted above). Is it really reward for sexual favors? Summarized, it certainly seems so (Boas 1935:185):

> A man appears and lies down with the young woman. The next day she hears the song of the bird of good luck. From now on she finds every day larger and larger animals under the bark of trees. The two women become rich, for all the tribes come to buy food from them.

In its unprecised form, however, the tone is quite different. The first morning it is a little squirrel, which the two women roast: "it was enough for one day for them" (1912:75):

> When it was morning again, she went again to the place where she had been before to get bark. She took again a very long means of breaking off bark. Then the bark fell down again. Then she gathered it up again. Behold! she found [again] a large grouse among the bark that she was gathering. She returned happy. Then she roasted it also; it was enough for them for one day.
>
> It was morning again, and the little noble woman went again; she went again to the foot of the large spruce tree where she had been before to gather bark. Again she took a very long stick to break off the bark. The bark fell down again, and she put it together again. Then she found a large porcupine. She took it down and gave it to her mother. Then her mother took the large porcupine. Then she burnt it over, and it was enough for them for two days.
>
> It was morning again, and she went again to gather bark. Then she found a large beaver among the bark. She took it down and gave it to her mother. Then her mother dried the meat of the beaver.
>
> It was morning again, and she went again to get bark. Then she found a large mountain-goat among the bark.

Squirrel, grouse, porcupine, beaver, mountain-goat: this is incremental jubilation far beyond a one-night stand. This is serious courting. But the suitor does not yet appear, only bigger animals falling with the bark out of the spruce tree. The next is a black bear, and they increase the size of their house (1912:77). Then a grizzly

bear; their house is full of meat. Then a caribou! One can just hear
the story-teller getting into this, so that there is actual laughter as
the next new bulky animal falls down, clunk, at the woman's feet.
Too tedious for our taste perhaps, geared as we are to the twenty-
second commercial. But such incremental repetition has enthralled
previous societies. The timing and mime as the oral narrator meets
fully the expectations of his audience through an ambling sequence
culminates with the revelation of the source of all this bounty—
again perhaps, from our point of view over-prepared for, and in
stilted conversation. But then we have to reckon with the charm of
the story-teller (1912:77, 79):

> Every morning before she went to gather bark, she
> heard [again] Hats!Enā's speak on the top of the large
> rotten spruce-tree. One morning she went up again to
> gather bark. Then she found a large caribou. Before she
> was about to call her mother, she heard a man going up
> to her from behind: therefore she suddenly turned
> around. Behold! a handsome young man stood near,
> behind her. All of a sudden she was much afraid.
>
> Then the handsome young man asked her, "What
> are you doing here?" Then the woman said to him, "Oh
> supernatural one! I (am beginning to) gather bark here.
> That is where I find animals every morning. Then I
> gather bark." Then the young man continued, and
> questioned the young woman: "Do you not know
> whence all the animals come that you have found?"
> Then the woman said, "No." Then the young man said
> to the woman, I am the one who has given to you the
> animals that you always find among the bark that you
> are gathering, and I am [he is] also the one who entered
> (your house) when you were beginning to sleep in your
> camp." That was when the young noble woman was
> glad [hollow in her heart].
>
> Then she was pregnant. He said, "Go and tell your

mother that I desire to marry you." Then the young
man promised every thing good to the woman. When
he finished speaking, he suddenly disappeared.
However, her mother came up to where she was, for she
had been away [lost] for a long time. Then her mother
asked her, "Why have you been away so long?"

It is in this manner that our hero Asdiwal is conceived; the embrace
of the gods is never fruitless.

Asdiwal is apparently destined to be a mountain man. His
father gives him "his bow and four arrows and a lance and a hat and
a cane and a basket and a bark rain-coat" (1912:81). And then he
disappears out of their lives, with the promise that he'll be there if
Asdiwal gets into difficulties. Good luck, and he is gone. (I believe
it was Norman Douglas who said that every father should arrange
to die when a son becomes fifteen.)

We now get the first episode of the grown-up Asdiwal, the
chasing of the white bear. This bear had evaded capture by other
villages. When it came to Asdiwal's (he and his mother having gone
down river to Canyon village) he put on the regalia his father had
given him and "ran in pursuit, as though a bird were flying"
(1912:83). Then there is a classic chase, where Asdiwal uses first his
lance, then his arrows, in order to bridge a chasm that the white
bear seems to be able to make at will by kicking the tops of
mountains. Asdiwal is taking on himself extraordinary powers
(1912:85, 87):

> When he saw the white bear running before him, he
> suddenly reached a great plain at the very end of the
> top of the mountain. After a good while, behold!
> Asdiwal suddenly saw a large ladder standing on our
> world. It stood on the top of the mountain (ridge)
> towards the sky. Behold! the white bear went up, and he
> followed it on the ladder. Then the man also went up.
> The white bear reached the top of the great ladder, and

Asdi-wā'l also suddenly reached the top. That was where the young man also reached the top of the great ladder. Then he found a great prairie. It was quite green with grass, and there were all kinds of flowers. Everything sweet-smelling was on the great prairie. It was that among which the little path lay. This was the one that the great white bear followed.

Then Asdl-wā'l also followed in the path. He kept the same distance; and behold! the path led to the outside of a great house, which stood across the way in the middle of the great prairie. The White bear suddenly went in, and Asdi-wā'l also suddenly reached [against] it. He stood against the door and looked in through a little hole. Behold! it was a young woman whom he had followed, and who took off her white-bear blanket and put it really away.

Then the great chief questioned the young woman, and said, "Did you not get what you went for, child"—"It is standing outside, behind the house," said the young woman. "I am almost dead with fatigue." Then said the chief, "Accompany him in."

This is the chief in heaven, the Sun. Asdiwal, it seems, has been chosen for a role larger than life. But if he thinks he can just settle in, he is very much mistaken. The rite of passage continues with what are known collectively as the son-in-law tests. (Twenty-three pages of *Tsimshian Mythology* are devoted to the forty-five separate tests gathered from all the analogues to this story, 1916:794-817.) Their popularity is no doubt due to the ingenuity of the son-in-law's escaping the father's clutches, but there are also psychological depths in the father's rivalry for his daughter and the way she immediately cleaves to the husband she has just met, warning him.[34] There are treacheries here that the printed word can hardly measure up to, compared with what an experienced raconteur can communicate by an aside (1912:89):

> Then Asdi-wā'l laughed. "Don't be afraid, [but] I myself have also great supernatural power." Thus he said to his wife. "Take care of yourself!" said his wife again. "This is what my father always does whenever I get married." Then Asdi-wā'l only laughed again.
>
> Then on the next morning the Chief spoke and said to his son-in-law, "My dear, say that I wish my son-in-law to go up for the mountain-goats there in the woods, because I desire mountain-goat meat and mountain-goat tallow." Then the princess said to her husband, "Do not go there. You will make a mistake if you do." Then Asdi-wā'l just laughed.

Part of what is going on here must be a play on Asdiwal's name. The Tsimshian word for "you will make a mistake," given on the opposing page (1912:88) is "me-asdi-wan-gin." The glossary (1912:257) gives "asdiwal" as a verb, "to be in danger," with the root "asdi-" indicating "by mistake."[35] So all through the length of the narrative we are waiting for Asdiwal to make his big mistake.

But he makes no mistake here. The trick he uses is to put his raincoat over his cane and his hat on top, so the stars think he is stuck. "Asdiwal cannot move, hau!" they chant. But he himself has escaped the fog and the earth tremors. The Kite star knows this, and is glad.

> Then just one star said, "No,'" he said, "only his cane is standing there. It has on his rain-coat, and it has on his hat, but he has gone over the top of the mountain." All the stars, however, disbelieved him. (That was the star that we call "The Kite," for we give names to all kinds of stars. It does not often twinkle, as several other stars do.) Then said the Kite star, "Asdi-wā'l has gone across."

Thus he said when the others began to say, "He cannot move." We will stop here.

"We will stop here": another flag denoting oral performance. We are indebted to Boas for leaving in this pre-literary marker, even though he makes no comment on its rarity and significance.

After the break the speaker gets going on a very familiar mytheme of these parts—Tate even has it later as a separate variant, "The Feast of the Mountain Goat" (1916 #12). Surely these had their origin in words to accompany pre-hunting ritual. When a song is involved one scents the archaic.

When Asdi-wā'l went over the ridge, behold! he saw a large house standing there in the middle of the great plain on top of the mountain. Then he heard a great noise of drums and a great noise of shamans. Then he went very slowly towards the great house. He looked in. Behold! a shaman mountain-goat was dancing [floating] around in a circle to see the future: therefore all the many mountain-goats had gone into the large house to hear what the shaman mountain-goat was going to say (about) what unfortunate event it was going to foresee. Then it ran around the fire [in the house] which was made to burn in the house, and all the many mountain-goats were beating time. One of them had a wooden drum in the corner.

When it was running around, it suddenly said, "Hi! I don't know why people disappear." When the shaman mountain-goat jumped over the great fire again, a little female lamb that followed behind the shaman mountain-goat also jumped over the fire: but all the mountain-goats beat time vigorously. Then they started their song. Asdi-wā'l was standing in the doorway, and he held his weapons ready. When the first song was

ended, they began another song. Then the shaman
mountain-goat said again, "Hi! the people vanish, hau!"
When he jumped over the fire again, then the lamb also
did so behind him.

"Smell of Asdi-wā'l and smell of shamans, he!"

When the song said "Smell of Asdi-wā'l smell of
shamans!" the shaman mountain-goat jumped right
over his head, and the little lamb jumped over the head
of Asdi-wā'l; but then Asdi-wā'l clubbed all the
Mountain-goats. Not one was saved.

The lamb is set up to be saved, as he is in some analogues, but
Asdiwal in the midst of son-in-law tests has no time for lambs. He
has to butcher the "several hundred mountain-goats" (1912:93)
and get the belly fat home to pile it in front of them all. The chief
is rather poker-faced about it, and just goes on to the next test. If
this were a written narrative there would have to be some reaction
shown; here the narrator probably just ground his teeth.

The second test is a Symplegades, a cave that opens and closes
with deadly clashing rocks. Asdiwal sends in a slave first. Splash,
there goes the slave. Then Asdiwal can get in quick and bring back
some of the spring water. This time the father-in-law was rather
disconcerted. So he brought the slave back to life.

The third test is a close repeat of the second, but with a rotten
tree. Asdiwal again gives the slave his freedom; and the chief has to
bring him back to life.

The fourth test is bad; Asdiwal is out of his element
(1912:103):

When, however, Asdi-wā'l lay down with his wife, she
said to him, "Only one (thing) is left with which my
father is going to try you. That is his very last

supernatural power. He will bake you in his fire, and
will put you in the fire on stones when they are hot,
and place you on them." Then Asdi-wā'l did not say
anything, and cried the whole length of the night.

The chief should have had the slave stoke the fire, but that
spartican turn of the wheel was not apparently something even Tate
could think of. But the fire was indeed stoked, while as for Asdiwal
he dawdles at the back of the house. It is here his father Hatsenas
(Good Luck) fulfills his promise. The solution to the problem is
simple: pieces of ice under the armpits. Fight fire with ice. It works.
He comes out unscathed, even leaving some of the embers frozen
(1912:107).

Then the chief said, "Indeed, you have really greater
supernatural power than I, son-in-law." Thus said the
chief, who is the Sun, to his son-in-law. Now he liked
his son-in-law much, and he respected him.

This reversal of fortune is standard, but I have trouble with this
punk Asdiwal beating out the Sun. Who do these Eagles think they
are?[36] This cockiness contains the seeds of tragedy.

There is this about Native traditional stories as they come down
to us: they don't take much time on character development.
Asdiwal is not made personally attractive as a hero. He's a great
hunter. OK. He has a few tricks up his sleeve. This seems to be
enough for the traditional Native audience. It must be the way the
old story-tellers filled out these characters so that feelings flowed
toward them: that must be it. Personally, after the mother and
daughter leave the story I find nobody to root for. Having said
that, I also have to say that we are drawn on by any drama,
regardless of the sympathy we may or may not have with the
characters. Somebody wants something, and he or she is prevented
from getting it. We have to know what happens, whether the
characters are finely drawn or not. This is the basic stuff: ambition,

revenge, desire for a loved one, or what the Welsh, who are experts in this matter, call *hiraeth*, homesickness (1912:109):

> Then one day again Asdi-wā'l was homesick for those whom he had left behind on our world. Then he was downhearted and thought how it was. Then he told his wife. After some time the Chief saw how his son-in-law was, that he was heavy at heart. Therefore he questioned him. Then the young woman told him that her husband was homesick; and the chief said, "The place you left behind is not far, son-in-law. You shall go there."

Personal success is as nothing unless it can be registered with one's own people. The descent from heaven is, indeed, easy, like a simple change of attention. Asdiwal and his wife walk into a winter village, which is again in the throes of starvation; he brings to his mother much food and prestige, so that he gets from her a new name: Potlatch-Giver.

Then follows an intermezzo. The sun's daughter has a plume which, when dipped in freshly drawn water, will indicate faithfulness on the part of the husband. It is an adultery detector, and of course Asdiwal one day allows himself to respond to the smile of another, and when the plume turns the water into slime Princess Evening-Star hits him in the face with it and goes off up a sunbeam, home. Asdiwal falls off the ladder "and was entirely gone" (1912:113). This may very well be one of the "situations that are appealing even outside the range of North West Coast culture" but it does nothing for the unity of the story. At the end of this episode we are exactly where we were three pages before, for the father-in-law Sun revives Asdiwal with his net, domestic harmony in heaven is resumed for a time, homesickness sets in, and they again travel down to the village as before. Sheer repetition, just to get the plume business in; and the plot has to be jerked forward by two arbitrary events, the death of the mother and the strangely casual disappearance of the heaven-wife: "she suddenly disappeared, and he did not see her again" (1912:115). Maybe this is true to life. I don't know. It just seems to be an expedient device to free Asdiwal to go down river and marry again.

Which he does. These are what I would call "bits." Oral performance is made up of formulaic units. Within the framework of Asdiwal's questing, we have had the white bear bit, three father-in-law tests, including the mountain goats bit, we have had the homesickness bit twice in order to get in the plume litmus test. I have the feeling that an oral narrator could have used very different selections from his repertoire of "bits" and still have got us to the same point. Yet these particular ones are chosen with some dexterity; they all pertain to the mountain and ice theme. The plume business on the face of it does not fit, but essentially Asdiwal is, in this bit as in the others, flirting with danger, a point which is driven home when, in an analogue in Barbeau's *Totem Poles*, Asdiwal follows the insulted princess, repeating, "Come back, come back, I have made a mistake, come back!" (1950:141).

The whole story, I think, will prove to be unified by that word "mistake" imbedded in the hero's name: pride before a fall. The second part is all hubris. I say "second part" because I assume this is where Boas sees the division of the "two independent parts"—although he gives no indication in his one-paragraph paraphrase of the story (Boas 1935:186):[37]

> His faithfulness is tested by his wife who has a feather
> which turns water into slime when her husband as
> much as looks upon another woman. When this
> happens she leaves him walking across the ocean. He
> follows, but when she looks back he sinks. Her father
> fishes up his bones and revives him. Again he becomes
> homesick. His wife disappears and he returns to earth.
> Now he marries the sister of four brothers. They
> become jealous on account of his success in bear
> hunting and leave him. Another party finds him and

again be marries the sister of four brothers. With his brothers-in-law be goes sealion hunting wearing his snowshoes, lance and bow and kills sealions. His brothers-in-law are jealous of his prowess and desert him against the wishes of the youngest one.

Far from unification, what we have here is awkward repetition. Asdiwal marries a woman with four brothers and alienates them by showing off his prowess as a mountain hunter as opposed to their seahunting. He then marries a woman with four brothers and gets into a similar sort of altercation. If Boas thinks that repetition of a theme is a factor in unification I cannot agree: only disparate things can be unified. What happens with the first set of brothers-in-law seems to be just a warm-up for what happens with the next set. It's unnecessary. Is it a happenstance of the oral method or is it an inept deliberateness? We should note that Tate never revised narratives, never crossed out paragraphs, in his manuscripts. His writing these stories down is a little like oral performance in that respect: what is said is there, and cannot be erased, even if off track. The first sister of four brothers becomes pregnant but moves on with them during the night and we do not see the birth; but we do see the birth of a son to the second sister of four brothers. Asdiwal kills four bears in the first act of competitiveness, and kills four bears a page later with the second group. This is not presented as remarkable. I think Tate got off to a wrong start and rectified it without deletion or comment. Why not? Is there some compulsion for us to see these stories as flawless?

What Tate's version is getting on to—and analogues go directly to (Boas 1916:817)—is the sea-lion rock episode, which is of interest because Asdiwal applies his mountain climbing skills to scaling sea-swept rocks and doing mass slaughter on the sea-lions, which achievements put his brothers-in-law to shame. The eldest brother orders his canoe away, and the other brothers follow suit, the youngest with extreme reluctance (noted later when revenge is meted out). Asdiwal has made another mistake because of pride.

He survives on the rock alone for two or three days partly because of his own ingenuity but in the final extremity because his father Good Luck again saves him, this time with a blanket against the cold (ice theme).

We then have a very popular "bit": Asdiwal is invited below into the caverns of the sea where he "cures" sick sea-lions by pulling out arrows invisible to them. These are his own arrows, so it's a rather cheap ride. In gratitude, the sea-lion chief sends the hero home in an inflated stomach. It's a popular tale. I don't know whether Boas liked it.

Boas should at least have commented on an interesting stylistic interruption, a "meanwhile" paragraph, prolonging the suspense and swerving to a different angle on the event (1912:131, 133):

> ...all the sea-lions loved Potlatch-Giver because he had saved them from the epidemic. He staid for some time in the house of the sea-lions. Now we will go no further with what Potlatch-Giver did.

> As soon as the great storm subsided, the four brothers-in-law desired to visit the rock to see whether their brother-in-law was dead or alive. Therefore one morning they arose and went to the rock. They stood on it, but they did not find him. Therefore they thought that the waves had knocked him off, when the great waves went along all day during the great storm. Then they returned to the shore. The wife of Potlatch-Giver cried all the time because her husband was dead. Every morning she carried her child on her back and went with it into the woods, crying all day long. And when it was really dark, she entered again.

> Now we will return again to Potlatch-Giver.

This kind of attempted montage is rare among the mainly paratactic narratives and, though rudimentary, deserves comment. It prepares us for what Asdiwal will see on his return, the surprise of the brothers and the relief of the wife. One thing it fails to do is distinguish between the callous older brothers and the remorseful youngest brother. This genuine lapse should not go unnoted. This passage could have reinforced what is stressed later when Asdiwal asks his wife, "Have those who are your brothers looked after you well?" and she replies, with "No, only the youngest one sympathizes with me; but his elder brother hates him because he loves me" (1912:137). That settles it. We now know who will have to die. I will not recount how Asdiwal accomplishes his revenge, but safe to say a rough eye-for-an-eye justice is meted out. The sister and remaining brothers take it all very decently. Or so we must presume, for Asdiwal stays on there without incident for a year.

> After one year, one day he wished to return to those
> whom he had left behind on the Skeena River.
> Therefore he started, and left his wife and his child. He
> was alone in his canoe. He steered for a town
> G·înadâ′⁰s; that was where he staid for a while. There
> he made again a great potlatch. Then he took again a
> chief's name. Stone-Slinger (Da-huk-dza′n) was his new
> name.

> After he had given his potlatch, his eldest son by his
> first wife came. He was a young man and a very great
> hunter. He asked for the bow and the arrows of his
> father. Therefore Stone-Slinger gave them to him, and
> the boy also gave a little dog to his father. Then they
> parted. The boy was an expert hunter.

> When it was fall again, Stone-Slinger arose and went up
> to the lake of G·înadâ′⁰s to hunt mountain-goats.

When he got up to the lake, behold! mountain-goats
were all about like grubs on one side of the mountain.
Then he took the little dog which his son had given to
him, and his lance, and he went up the mountain, and
he stabbed the mountain-goats. At last he let the
mountain-goats slide down.

After a short while, he remembered that he had
forgotten his snowshoes in his house; then he could not
move on the great slippery mountain, for he had
forgotten his snowshoes, which he always used in
difficulties; for with these snowshoes he succeeded in all
difficulties, wherever it might be. Therefore what could
he use now? He only carried his dog about which his
son had given to him. Therefore he always stood there.
Where might he go now? He could not go up, he could
not go down, he could not go to either side.

After a little while, his father, Hū'⁰t, came. It was he
who went away with him to his own home, but his
body staid behind and became stone; also the little dog
and the lance, all became stone; and even now they
stand there on the very top of the great mountain at the
lake of G·înadâ'⁰s; and the whole number of
generations of people have seen him standing there on
the mountain. He and his dog and his lance are stone.
This is the end.

This ending (1912:143, 145) violates any unity the second part
may have. It is an epilogue to the whole, and shows Asdiwal, true
to his name at last, making a mistake in forgetting his magic snowshoes which proves fatal.

There is a certain neatness to this denouement, but it also contains quite a few loose ends. There is no motivation for Asdiwal to
move to a different village. Why the "eldest son by his first wife"
(1912:143) has to appear is not at all clear—except to provide an

advertisement for a sequel (Tate supplies such, on request, in the story "Waux, the Son of Asdiwal" where the son, like the father, ends up transfixed on a mountain because "he forgot to take his spear" 1916:246). The little dog has no function in the story—it's just that the local people can see a dog up there on the mountain with Asdiwal. The change of name to "Stone-Slinger" also serves no apparent purpose. Boas gives a footnote suggesting there is a relation to the Nass word for "Evening sky" (1912:143), but there is no comment on how that might conceivably help us to understand the adoption of the name. The father's name too is a puzzle, changed without explanation from Hatsenas to Hut.

I believe there is a level on which these problems transmute into something valuable. But it is not the level on which Boas is offering a literary judgment when he says (1935:186), "Although the story consists of two independent parts each is well unified and based on situations that are appealing even outside the range of North West Coast culture." On this level the story is far from being what Boas claims it to be, and it is perplexing to think that he could chose it for praise of this sort. The two "parts" are not at all "well unified." The unification comes in understanding the story as a whole. There are not two "independent parts." How could there be, when we have here a biography of a person whose actions overall demonstrate one ruling passion? Any one of the "bits" that make up the story is independent in the sense that it can be dropped and one still has an Asdiwal story. For instance, in Chief Mountain's telling of the white bear episode, Asdiwal gets only as far as the door where the people are singing and is "unable to enter" (1902:228). I don't know if this is what Boas meant by "independent." He seems to have the concept of two independent parts, each unified in itself, and tacked on to each other without any necessity (otherwise they would be dependent parts). I don't see how Boas can propose to analyze the story in this simplistic way, and I certainly don't see how he can praise it on the basis of this analysis.

Boas's other criterion, that the story is "appealing even outside the range of North West Coast culture," is equally ridiculous.

What can possibly be appealing to us in a pasteboard supernatural who takes advantage of starving women and abandons his role as parent for no good reason; what can possibly be appealing to us in a father-in-law trying his best to kill his daughter's new husband without knowing him; what can possibly be appealing about four men deserting their companion on a sea-lion rock just because he proved himself a better hunter than they, or the abandoned one concocting a revenge where he manufactures magic killer-whales to do the job for him while he stays completely out of danger? These are the main themes of the Asdiwal story and they are mightily unappealing to us—unless. Unless we do exactly what Boas says is not necessary in this case: enter into North West Coast culture and try to come close to the reason why literature alien to us can be appealing to other human beings differently placed. Maybe Boas meant to say "intriguing," for we are intrigued even by some things not comfortable enough to appeal to us. Anthropologists and others of curious mind are especially intrigued when the matter at hand is obdurately attached to ritual and half forgotten legacies of formerly viable cultures. Not that we want to dwell on the difficulties that poorly told stories present, but sometimes the highest tribal art comes in a strange and difficult form.[38]

It is not within the scope of this book to undertake the job of plumbing the depths of the mystery that the Asdiwal story's paradoxical nature entails. It would take the application of a lifetime of commitment in order to get beneath the surface of it. If I complain about Boas it is because he was the one who should have done it, and he didn't. Take a simple moment of tension like the brother confronting Asdiwal's wife as she takes the box of tools out of the house. He wants to know what she is doing. She has a quick answer ready: she is going to burn it. That this answer satisfies the questioner would hardly make sense unless we were aware that he accepts her intention is not to destroy the tools wastefully but to make them part of a funeral ritual. Her deception cleverly makes use of a socially approved act of "burning" and any suspicion is allayed. There is nice irony in the fact that, as Beynon says in a note to his revision of this section, "this is burning a possession of the deceased person in order to convey it to them by fire."[39] She is conveying the box to a living husband, pretending he is dead in order to hoodwink the intended victim. The text is more exciting when the reader knows what is really going on. Boas, as is his wont, chooses not to provide this kind of helpful footnote. He hides the clue away in the "Description of the Tsimshian, Based on Their Mythology" section, where he notes, "Sacrifices are offered at the grave. Thus a widow gets her dead husband's tool box to burn it" (1916:443). This is droll: instead of a footnote where the drama and irony can be felt, we get, in isolation, a supposed fact, which is no fact at all. She is not a widow and is not going to burn the tool-box. Boas separates his explications from any questioning moment of the reader's experience with the text. Without this connection they lose much of their usefulness and become, if not actual mis-statements, mere drab talk.

Again, anyone in Tate's narrator's audience would know what the little dog is for. Little dogs upon the enunciation of a magical formula can become big hounds and aid in the hunt. This happens in other stories, and the idea is present here even if nothing happens. Some archetypal hound-dog feeling from the loam of the story-telling tradition is there for those who are in the know.

But most of us aren't. What we are most in need of in order to read these tales aright is probably a reverence for the workings of the natural world, which includes the supernatural at every point. We need a radical apprenticeship into what is possible as explication and literary criticism of the Native oral corpus. I am disappointed with Boas for not pushing us toward this essential reeducation. On the one occasion when he proposes to speak about the value of a story, he chooses to talk about unified plots and appealing situations, when the real work to be done is on a different plane entirely.

We need to salvage the archaic substratum of a story like "Asdiwal." The connection must be back to the whole hunting ethos, the technical preparations for success, the rehearsal of privations, the psychological states of mind that bring animals into the hunter's vicinity and power. In an analogue to the story, the mother and daughter, on first hearing of the call of the bird of good fortune, "began to pray and sacrificed red paint, eagle feathers and inner cedar bark as it is used for dancing ornaments, to him. They threw all this into the fire" (Boas 1895:283). Tate includes this ritual later when the wife wants to aid the efficacy of the killer-whale carving with a burnt sacrifice of "food and fat and down of birds and red ochre" (1912:139). We have noted other evidences of antiquity in Tate's version, especially the song of the mountain goats (1912:93), which has no plot function and must be a vestige of a hunter's rationale.

Who knows how much of the story's epilogue is there for reasons now forgotten? The meeting with the firstborn son may have archaic compulsions. The exchange of gifts may mark a generational treachery, the weakening of the father, the son the executioner. It triggers Asdiwal's tragic flaw, the great "mistake" that has been hovering over him all his life. It is an improbable alzheimer thing for him to "forget" his snowshoes.[40] Fate brings on the very thing that, in one's right mind, one would avoid easily. Oedipus so forgot himself as to kill someone old enough to be his father and marry someone old enough to be his mother. Ginadas village is a world away from the Corinthian peninsula, but a similar notion of nemesis seems to be at work. Asdiwal, very much like Oedipus at Colonus, is taken away into the spirit world, an escape with his father (whose new name Hut means "escape," according to Boas's glossary 1912:262), leaving his frozen body to be a sign to future generations. I have not found where Boas deals with this apotheosis in his "Description of the Tsimshian" section; in any case, it is just a shame that he could not offer his knowledge at the moment we need it and in a manner which gives these stories a chance to exercise their full hidden power. What does it mean to have Asdiwal and his dog on top of the mountain above your village?

Claude Lévi-Strauss has an answer to the question. Asdiwal and his dog constitute figures of mediation between two poles, tempering the contradictions which produce social tension: this, whether, as a villager of Ginadas, you know it or not. For the basic premise of Lévi-Strauss's work is that the structuralist knows better than the story-teller what the story is doing.

For instance Lévi-Strauss makes a great deal of the movements of Asdiwal up and down the Skeena and the Nass rivers imposing the schema N S E W, which would never have entered the mind of a Tsimshian. Where Lévi-Strauss abstracts compass directions from these journeys, I see rather an attempt by Tate to give a picture of the known Tsimshian world in somewhat the same way as Homer used a portulans and created a Mediterranean geography through Odysseus' adventures. I stand by a human world, not a diagram.

My whole approach to myth and legend is so diametrically opposed to that of Lévi-Strauss I would not know where to begin if other critics had not already largely demolished his structuralist pretensions.[41] I refer chiefly to L.L. Thomas, J. Z. Kronenfeld and D. B. Kronenfeld, "Asdiwal Crumbles: a Critique of Lévi-Straussian Myth Analysis" in *American Ethnologist* 3 (February 1976: 147-173), from which I cull the following:

> Lévi-Strauss' emphasis on strict dichotomies in his schema, for example, high/low (heaven/earth), can be seen to be gross simplification of the story... The arbitrariness we find in the "integrated" geographical and cosmological schema will show that the simplifications are quite possibly not useful... Given the nature of his implicit supporting evidence, Lévi-Strauss' argument is no more compelling than it would be with no supporting evidence at all. His "proof" proves nothing... In any case, no clarification is offered; it is not the responsibility of the reader to tease it out.

These criticisms are mildly stated (from my point of view) but the cool examination they summarize is devastating.

I take one example only, a crux in Lévi-Strauss's argument that is so wrong as to be catastrophic for his whole system (and it is so obvious that I was aware of it before I read the above article pp. 152-53). The exact position of Asdiwal's demise is of utmost importance to Lévi-Strauss's duplexity (p. 19):

```
┌High
│              ┌ Water
└Low ─┤                    ┌ Sea-hunting
            └ Land ─┤                              ┌Peak
                         └ Mountain-hunting ─┤
                                                    └Valley
```

Lévi-Strauss has everything in double-harness. Don't ask me to explain this plausible nonsense, but in its own terms clearly everything depends on Asdiwal ending "at zero point (half-way up, between peak and valley)" (p. 20). Lévi-Strauss quotes the penultimate paragraph of the story (1912:145): "Where might he go now? He could not go up, he could not go down, he could not go to either side." This might indicate that Asdiwal was "trapped half-way up the mountain-side" (Lévi-Strauss p. 17). But Lévi-Strauss does not quote the final paragraph of the story: "all became stone; and even now they stand there on the very top of the great mountain at the lake of Ginadas" (1912:145). The very top: Lévi-Strauss cannot get around that "very top." So, like the unabashed juggler he is, he ignores the dropped ball. He bluffs it out like a true Boasian.

Chapter Eight

It was Franz Boas who enunciated the principle that Claude Lévi-Strauss extended with much intricate chicanery, the principle that myths can provide insight into the culture of primitive societies. Lévi-Strauss credits Boas with a daring innovation: "it is always rash to undertake, as Boas wanted to do in his monumental *Tsimshian Mythology*, 'a description of the life, social organization and religious ideas and practices of a people...as it appears from their mythology'" (Lévi-Strauss 1967:29). But Boas apparently is not rash enough. "The myth is certainly related to given (empirical) facts," Lévi-Strauss continues, "but not as a *representation* of them. The relationship is of a dialectic kind, and the institutions described in the myths can be the very opposite of the real institutions. This will in fact always be the case when the myth is trying to express a negative truth" (1967:29). We cannot follow Lévi-Strauss any further into this; if he wants to dive off a high board into three inches of reality, then let him. Boas at least believes in the notion of common sense, even if he wanders away from it from time to time. For instance, talking about how myths reveal relationships, he says: "The incident in which a man kills his Bear brother-in-law (282) can hardly be used in this connection" (1916:423-424). The reason is common sense: "because obviously it contains supernatural elements." But Boas cannot abandon his principle that easily. The killing of the Bear brother-in-law, even if it is pure fantasy, must be helpful ethnographically: "still," he has to say, "it is a reflection of the fact that quarrels between a man and his wife's brothers were not uncommon." It reflects no such thing. A bear has abducted the sister. Anybody would get excited. If Boas for one second thinks he might use this "Girl Who Married A Bear" fable as a clue to the nature of domestic tension among the Tsimshian—as he unfortunately does—then he opens the gate for Lévi-Strauss to perform all of his high dive back flips.

These are *stories*, not Rorschach tests where the hidden neuroses of a people are going to reveal themselves to professors. The movement properly goes quite contrary to that which Boas suggests. We should not gut the stories for supposed empirical evidence for tribal traits; instead we should bring to the stories all the wisdom about human nature, both universal and tribal, that we have at our disposal. The meaning resides first and foremost in the context of the narrative event. There is a very interesting moment in the bear story mentioned above (1916 #43). The Bear husband knows he will be killed and that his wife's brother will come to do it. When the brother comes, the sister says, "Now, my dear, do not kill your brother-in-law with knife, spear, or arrow. Just make a smudge in front of the den" (1916:282). The young man's reply is unexpected. He says, "I will not kill him." The sister says, "No, not so, my brother! Kill him, only do not use your spear if you kill him, that you may not die." There must be an archaic element here not fully expressed, but which may be part of the bear ceremonial rituals of all circumpolar areas. How does Boas handle this in his "Description of the Tsimshian, Based on Their Mythology"? Most inadequately, I would say. "Bears were smoked out of their dens and either suffocated (283) or killed with the spear (244, 1.119)" (1916:402). That's the trouble with this "Description of the Tsimshian" section; Boas seems to pick out only the most pedestrian stuff. What does he say about the brother's initial refusal to kill the Bear husband? Nothing. Yet it is most intriguing. The courtesies are very pronounced all through this story. The young man's willingness to abandon what he had prepared himself to do is an offer that grants every courtesy to the animal world, that respects its claim on us. It moves toward the unfathomable, and Boas apparently wants nothing to do with it. In fact, he changes Tate's manuscript "I will not kill him" (Columbia p. 745) to "I will kill him," which is how we find it published in *Tsimshian Mythology* (1916:282). Boas makes very few emendations (except in sexual parts), and yet he was compelled to leave out Tate's "not." There must have been a strong motive for doing such a thing. Even if on one level he had convinced himself that he was correcting a mere mistake, surely he must have felt some deeper prohibition in his act?

But then again, probably not. I don't think Boas had the foggiest idea what to do with the fictional. Here is what he gets out of the second part of the Asdiwal story: "The sea hunter required a training quite different from that of the mountain hunter." A platitude, indeed. "For this reason it is considered remarkable that a man from up river who settles among the island tribes becomes their best sea hunter" (1916:403). It is considered more than remarkable, downright offensive—but only in the story. It never happened anywhere else. And then we get Boas at his tangle-foot worst: "it is of course only a mythical incident if he used snowshoes on the slippery sea-lion rocks" (1916:403). Right, a mythical incident, right. What else is all that he is analyzing here? The way it turns out is that anything interesting in these stories is not capable of being used in the "Description of the Tsimshian" section; only the dull stuff is sifted out and stated with all appropriate objective flatness.

In the story "The Prince Who Was Deserted" (1916 #32), a chief orders the whole village to move and leave his son behind because of a supposed solecism that shames the family. There are many analogues to this story, and it really does not seem to matter what the offense is. It is usually something small: personal uncleanliness, bullying other children, cheating on a spirit quest, begging food from neighbours, general laziness. King Lear had better reasons than these for his mad banishment of Cordelia. In this case, the chief's son is feeding eagles all summer instead of storing salmon for the winter (1916:225). The youth has an attitude, but does it deserve the death penalty? Boas does not raise this lack of proportion between crime and punishment; instead, he uses a very matter-of-fact tone to bring it to our attention: we "find numerous cases in which a chief is displeased with his child of whom he is ashamed for one reason or another. On 225 the son will not work. When the strain becomes great, the father deserts the child" (1916:427). I have tried in vain to determine whether or not Boas thought that the Tsimshian actually had the practice of leaving children to certain death because of trifles. Is it known that parental annoyance sometimes took this form? Did it ever? I doubt it myself, and there seems to be no ethnographic evidence for it. Boas chooses to present this trait as part of his "Description of the Tsimshian, Based on Their Mythology" regardless of the lack of collaborative information. He repeats the point in a later paragraph: when a prince acts "in a way unbecoming to a member of the nobility, he may be deserted by his father. This happens when a prince, instead of catching salmon, makes arrows and feeds the eagles with salmon that ought to be stored for winter use" (1916:432). If Boas was willing to treat snowshoes on sea-lion rocks as beyond belief, why was he not able to do likewise here and say, "Of course this is too fantastic to be taken seriously, it's just myth." I sense that he secretly approves of strong measures to keep adolescents in line.

The deserted child is one of the most moving themes present throughout the whole area, and we would, indeed, like to know what is going on here. Did not Boas have enough time for a conversation with George Hunt on the topic, which might have gone something like this?

> Boas: Did you ever hear of a village leaving a child to
> die as a punishment?
> Hunt: Only in stories.

Boas: Do you think it happened in the distant past?
Hunt: I don't know.
Boas: Why do you think there are so many stories about
it?
Hunt: I don't know.

There is no such conversation on record, but one wishes there
were. Then we would see Boas doing his job, not sloughing off
responsibility, as he does here, merely repeating what's in the stories
as though it were reliable gossip. Again, in *Kwakiutl Culture As
Reflected in Mythology*, on the basis of Kwakiutl and Tsimshian
myth, Boas says: "we find among both tribes the desertion of
children who are disliked for one reason or another" (1935: 174-
175). I hope some day experts in the field will address this
particular point. Meanwhile, I shall choose to believe that this
popular motif, rather than a vestige of past atrocities, is a
constantly renewable image of a universal psychic condition, that
of alienation, the feeling of being abandoned, which this fiction
places before us for our feelings to attach themselves to and work
on.

Our final judgment on the "Description of the Tsimshian,
Based on Their Mythology" must be that it is essentially misguided
in its methodology. As it stands, it is just a product of uncritically
shuffling a thousand slips of paper under subject headings such as
"Towns, Houses, Household Goods, and Manufactures," "Dress
and Ornament," "Fishing, Hunting, and Food-Gathering,"
"Playing and Gambling," "Quarrel and War," "Social
Organization," "Family Life" and so on, in an uninspiring
sequence. The occasional editorial comments, as we have seen, are
on the dismal level of "The man who has eighteen Wolf children
belongs, of course, in the domain of myth" (1916:420). But it is *all*
in the domain of myth, and should be treated as such. Collected as
"information," it merely produces obvious saws such as "Patience
and persistence in pursuits are rewarded" (1916:444) with
sometimes self-contradictory statements, e.g. "During a famine the

rich people would leave the poor; and widows, old people, and orphans would die of hunger" (1916:399); "Noble youths only chew a little fat during a famine, and a noble family eats but very little" (1916:444); and all the time, missing the point that stories are things valuable in themselves.[42]

In any case, there are not enough stories in the total sample to provide statistically valid generalizations. A handful—a dozen at the very most—on any one theme is not enough. Any conclusion from that number might be totally refuted by the next several stories to be discovered and examined. A case in point is provided by Marius Barbeau in his review of *Tsimshian Mythology*. Barbeau notes (1917:554) one of Boas's major deductions from the mythology as given in the "Conclusion" to "Comparative Study of *Tsimshian Mythology*," the large section IV of *Tsimshian Mythology*: "the Tsimshian take a somewhat exceptional position among neighbouring tribes, and seem to be recent intruders on the coast" (1916:872). The chief origin legend behind this induction is "Gauo" (1912 #3, previously discussed), which is set in Temlaxam, or Prairie Town, the "original home of the Tsimshian" (1916:394— see also 1916:483, 486, 524, 525, quoted by Barbeau). "This thesis, however, is not entirely borne out by the facts at our disposal," says Barbeau, who ends up flatly contradicting Boas on the basis that the "Gauo" story is claimed by, and therefore gives the origin of, only a few families, a minority of the phratry which contains other clans with different origin crests. Some of these latter, sea-coast origin clans, says Barbeau, "convey the firm impression of being very ancient. The Temlaxam clan, it is considered by natives, are fairly recent intruders among the Tsimshian, being an offshoot of the interior Gitskan nation" (1917:554). Barbeau, through Beynon, has done a broad census: "while about 33 Tsimshian social units admit having Gitskan ancestors, this is denied of nearly 193 others. The proportion of 33 to 193, therefore, represents well the size of the interior elements that grafted themselves upon the already existing Tsimshian nation" (1917:555). Barbeau goes further and suggests that, rather than interior people coming down and founding the coast Tsimshian, the interior Tsimshian presumably migrated from the coast. By having more narratives at his disposal Barbeau can contradict one of Boas's slenderly supported main assertions.

Barbeau says nothing about the story "The Deluge" (1916 #61), which purports to tell of the original trek of the Tsimshian from the interior to the sea and the hooking of their first halibut. He would undoubtedly aver that this story too is claimed only by that same small minority, who probably did make such a journey back after coming originally from the coast in the first place, having as a group forgotten that they did.

This raises the age question, another great flaw in the claim that myths can give accurate insight into culture. We have no way of proving, except in unusual cases, how old a story element might be. Homer gave a specific place and date to his epic action, though there is some doubt that Troy was in fact the location of the "Trojan" War. The Tsimshian as well as most North American peoples have narratives that can be related to historical events, but the legends we are talking about with "Gauo" and most of the others are in a different category. Let us remind ourselves that story-tellers have been on this coast for probably ten thousand years at least. Perhaps there was once a "Deluge" in reverse which told of a shaman leading his people away from starvation on the coast to kill its first strange creature called a mountain goat. There was time for the Tsimshian to have a cannibal myth and then lose it. There was interaction with neighbours and even far-away visitors (including voyageurs) at all times. Boas in the name of science pins down this flux at a certain moment in time and pretends to be able to discern tribal character from the spray that history has thrown up through the agency of one man, Mr. Tate. That one person can speak for the tribe and that myths reflect cultural attitudes at the time they were collected: these are the two unsound pillars of Boas's faith. One informant is *not* enough; fifty are perhaps enough if one has lived in a place for two winters, as McIlwraith did in Bella Coola.[43] And myths have ancient, collective elements, and their archaic universal qualities are attractive to tellers and listeners who may be living by quite diverse mores.

I'm not saying that interesting conjectures, as conjectures, cannot be made in a broad way about the state of aboriginal myth by area in North America; for instance, the connection of the Raven cycle with Siberian examples of it or the way the trickster figure changes from Raven to Mink to Blue Jay and to Coyote as one goes down the coast to California. One does not have to be blinkered, but passages like the following are suspect, implying a taxonomic subtlety that is unjustified (1916:872): "Most remarkable among the inland stories found among the Tsimshian is that of the brothers who become sun and moon (p. 727), which has direct relationship to the corresponding tales of the Shuswap, Lower Thompson Indians, Okanagon, Kutenai, Wishram, and Wasco, but which has no analogue whatsoever on the North Pacific coast." QED. The Tsimshian, therefore, must have come from the interior. Boas's pet theory rests on this kind of flimsy support, where the words "direct relationship" seem to be carefully used because, though vague, they sound specific. We are talking here about the "Sun and Moon" story (1916 #8) that was discussed in chapter 2 and summarized there: "one of two teenage brothers made a pitch mask, ignited it and ran across the sky before it burnt out. He was at first a bit quick, so his sister regulated things by holding him in the middle of his journey. That's why the sun stops briefly at midday." I have looked at the interior stories that Boas terms "corresponding" and I find no correspondence at all, no "direct relationship" either. There is no pitch mask, no sister who holds the sun at midday. They are all animal stories about rivalry to become the sun and moon. Tate has no rivalry; the tone is more of an Aesop's fable to explain quasi-reasonably how sun, moon, stars, and fog came into being. Of course, the interior stories have nothing about fog. They are dissimilar in detail, in plot, in tone, in essence. One seriously has to doubt Boas's perspicacity, and consequently his deductions from the distinctions he is making.

"We are dealing here with a continuous stream, that runs from the interior to the coast by way of the Skeena River" (1916:872-873). I don't believe it.[44]

What is this dissemination of myths theory, anyway, but a doomed attempt to turn into a science the most ordinary sorts of occurrences with infinite variables? Stories went everywhere. It's more impossible than oceanography, because it is human beings paddling canoes and talking by firelight. I like the yarn that Livingston Farrand told in his introduction to *Traditions of the Chilcotin Indians* (1900). He was under Boas's strict guidance during this Jesup expedition and wrote solemnly about the problems of dispersal of myth-themes and the "comparison with the mythologies of other tribes, which is, after all, the great object of the work" (1900:4), but then with the specific story "The Story of Waiwailus" Farrand reveals a human side to "myth dissemination" (1900:6):

> When this tale was first told the writer, it was
> recognized as being almost word for word the Bella
> Coola story of "Wawalis." Inquiry of the narrator as to
> where it had first been heard only brought out the
> assurance that it had always been known in the tribe,
> and was one of their oldest traditions. Repeated
> inquiries of different individuals elicited the same asser-
> tion; but finally certain of the older Indians agreed that
> they had first heard the tale in their younger days from
> a man who, though very old, was fortunately still living
> at the time of the writer's visit. When this old man was
> questioned, he immediately answered without hesita-
> tion, that when a child he had been captured by the
> Bella Coola, and had lived with them for several years
> before being restored to his tribe, and that during his
> captivity he had heard the story, and had brought it to
> his people on his return.

Anecdotes like this puncture the hot-air balloon by which laputan scientists might propose to see patterns of dissemination of myths. There will be Raven stories where there are ravens, there will be Coyote stories where there are coyotes; there are world-wide themes that may have local variations related to tribal conditions, or not related. What more can one say than this? As a scientist Boas tried at great length to claim more, but failed to get his enormous ballast off the ground. We are better off allowing ourselves to be drawn into the intricacies and depths of particular stories, their dramatic flow and meaning, their uniqueness. But this is something Boas had no interest in doing.

Epilogue

In the February 1989 issue of *American Ethnologist,* I published an article, "The Henry Tate-Franz Boas Collaboration on *Tsimshian Mythology*," which touched on most of the points made in this book. I expected it to cause a sensation; but nothing happened. Admittedly I did not come on with any fanfare, but there I was saying that *Tsimshian Texts* (1912) and *Tsimshian Mythology* (1916) were not "exactly the collection of authentic traditional myths that they have been taken for" (1989:161). Nobody batted an eye. I spoke of the "methodological tangles that arose in a particular instance of conducting field work by mail. The anthropologist felt he had to make specific requests; tales were sometimes supplied, we deduced, only because of the asking, shaped by the way they were asked for" (1989:161). There was no stir in the crowd at these revelations. "Perhaps misunderstanding instructions," I continued, "the informant sometimes utilized previously published texts. Probably at times, in view of the method of payment, he made up narratives rather than seek out traditional storytellers of the tribe." Nobody seemed to mind, not even when I said, "The fact that the stories, for one reason or another, came to be written in English first was awkward for the editor, who tried in one publication to work, with an intermediary, from the interlinear native language sentences alone, and in the second publication fell to using the

English alone, shifted into more standard English" (1989:161). I thought this would have left Boas's reputation in tatters. The only explanation I could come up with for the total silence in the face of this scandal was that Boas must have been, among the cognoscenti, discredited long ago, and that I was the last one to know.

It was clear I was wrong on the last point when I submitted to the *American Anthropologist* a paper—the gist of which comprises Appendix D below—where some suspicious activities of both Boas and Hunt were exposed, and the journal's chosen referees shot the thing down with mighty salvoes. Boasians closed ranks with a vengeance and the piece was not published.

How had the *American Ethnologist* article managed to get published, then? A letter from a friend in the field, a scholar of independent views, cut through to the quick of the matter when he wrote, "Don't you think your concluding paragraph is a bit of a whitewash of Boas?" This remark made me realise that I too had been pulling my punches, to spare the archetypal father.[45] I had actually gone so far as to say in that concluding paragraph of the article, "All these circumstances should not be taken, however, as reducing the worth of this extraordinary collaboration" (1989:161). Whitewash? Well, a bit of sophistry, maybe. I was speaking of literary value only: "Each story, considered individually, presents an interesting case of improvisation on Tate's part, as though he were on a tightrope between oral and literary storytelling. And the volumes together are the amazing ten-year output of a writer, whose talent would have been dormant without Franz Boas, and whose reputation will only be further enhanced by a closer scrutiny of the manuscripts behind the printed page" (1989:161). I was saving Boas's skin by featuring him as Tate's literary agent. Tate came out a hero, so could Boas really be a villain? No.

In ending my article on this uplifting note I was averting the reader's gaze from the wreckage which transmission difficulties had produced. *Porcupine Hunter and other Stories* (Talonbooks 1993) was my attempt to demonstrate how Tate's work might amaze us with its beauty and depth of feeling if it were presented well, with sympathetic commentary attentive to a reader's needs. I said in the introduction to that volume that I was "not concerned with detailing previous error, but with simply freeing Tate from the previous restraint" (1993:viii). Now, six years later, it seems that the time has come to look back at the "wreckage" and not be so forgiving as before. My opinion is—and I want there to be no mistake this time—that it was Boas's responsibility entirely to make sure the pitfalls were avoided. If he was suspicious of Tate's work he should have put his foot down and asked who the informants were for each of the stories. He should have been firm. Tate, on his part, was a 20¢-a-page man, a piece-worker. It was not his duty to read Boas's mind. He tried to please, but hoped he could please by doing it his way, which, even when he was told it was not orthodox, still felt right to him. Tate had a family, had to go out fishing, had to go up the Nass with everyone else for oolichan. He had to attend funerals; he was sometimes ill, near death, himself. He was alone in the project. He had writing paper from Boas and a candle he supplied himself. He went out sometimes to hear stories but, in the words of Marius Barbeau, Tate "shared in his compatriots' corrosive diffidence" (1917:553). He "was not in the habit of taking down the stories under dictation. He was loth to divulge to other natives that he was really writing them down at all. Our assistant Beynon knew only of his 'keeping a little book at home for those things'" (1917:561). We know that Tate sometimes, as a short cut, wrote things out from books his boss had sent as a model. Sometimes, we suspect, he wrote from memory what he thought stories had been like, sometimes making things up. The result was an eclectic grab-bag. No blame can be attached to this. Indeed, homogeneity is an idea imposed by Boas, who thought that if the stories didn't all look alike and sound alike they wouldn't count as data. The imposed uniformity of tone gives a fake air of authenticity, as does the massive apparatus of comparative scholarship with its arbitrary compartments and impossible-to-follow abbreviations.

If only Boas had not been so uptight. If only he had been more forthright from the start and stated emphatically, "Listen Mr. Tate. You don't get another red cent from me until I know exactly what you are doing, what you are filching from the texts I sent you, what you are writing off the top of your head and what are the real goods, the exact words of the old storytellers you know. And stop writing these pieces in English first, or no more money orders." Boas didn't say any of these things; he didn't lay the law down. He compromised himself, just in order to get anything at all from a Tsimshian. (What compromises have not been made sometimes to keep an informant talking?) If Boas had stuck to his guns, Tate might conceivably have turned around and produced some texts of traditional Tsimshian speech very much more satisfying in their authenticity.

But failing that rigorous approach, and having allowed Tate to send him what he did, what were Boas's duties as an editor? Rather than hide the problems, as he mainly did, Boas was duty bound to tell exactly what he knew or didn't know about the provenance of each story. Footnotes should have presented the analogues useful in giving a sense of the tradition Tate was working in; these matters should not have been reserved for a scholarly apparatus that outweighed the narratives themselves and gave a false seal of approval to texts of uncertain validity. Given that Tate wrote in English first and that his Tsimshian was a mere translation of that primary English text, Boas's duty was to publish the stories as close to Tate's English as reasonably possible. Wherever they individually may have come from, these stories are certainly well told and very attractive in their own movement and diction. Boas's *Tsimshian Mythology* has deadened these lively stories and ruined them for readers for over eighty years. It all has to be done over again to bring out Tate's unique value, and now done without the aid that Boas could have given us but didn't think to do because he was not interested in his informant's individual talent.

Notes

Notes

1   In the Boas festschrift, Jacobs 1959:120 and 126. Claude Lévi-Strauss also used the word "monumental"—or his translator did (Lévi-Strauss 1967:29). Marius Barbeau in his review of *Tsimshian Mythology* calls it "voluminous" (1917:548). The contributors of the "Tsimshian Peoples" chapter to the Northwest Coast volume of the *Handbook of North American Indians* use no adjective at all (Halpin and Seguin 1990:283).

2   Garfield 1953:32-34. Leslie Spier's analysis of *Tsimshian Mythology*, while noting that the "implication of this body of data is not directly discussed at any length by Boas" (Spier 1931:456), manages to roundly praise the volume: "This study is a characteristic example of the empirical methods of the school of American anthropologists founded by Boas. It embodies all that could be learned of the folk literature of one people. The analysis to show the history of the tales and their psychic content is the most thorough and consequential yet known" (Spier 1931:457).

3   Letter of 15 April 1903 in the library of the American Museum of Natural History (abbreviated AMNH).

4   A later Wellington Clah told the story to William Beynon in 1950 (MacDonald and Cove 1987, 2:210-212). See also Arctander 1909:133-134.

5   Thus the compiler of the Catalogue of Wellcome Americana p. 209; see Robin Price (1983).

6   Photograph from the British Columbia Archives and Records Service (P10727) reproduced following p. 68 in Bolt 1992. Unfortunately Tate is not mentioned by name (nor, I think, alluded to at all) in Thomas Crosby's memoir, see Crosby 1914.

7   Bolt 1992:53. Also see Ralph Maud, entry under "Tate, Henry Wellington" in *Dictionary of Canadian Biography*—Maud 1998.

8   Ridley 1903:105. We perhaps would know a great deal more about all this if there had not been a disastrous fire in 1901 in which practically all of Ridley's accumulated possessions went up in smoke, including "material for a book on the origin, habits, traditions, and religions of Indians" (Ridley 1903:191). The *Tsimshian Gospels* volume was published well before the fire, in 1886, by the Society for Promoting Christian Knowledge.

9   For the record, Boas is paraphrasing answers Tate gave to a question in a Boas letter of 12 March 1913 (American Philosophical Society, Philadelphia, abbreviated APS):

> My grant-father give his name to me thats my mother's father, and all his relation was gone. They call me his name now, and I fill his relationship. I am not Eagle now But I am Gishbou-wa-wada, and I am not able to married to Eagle woman but to raven relation. And still my uncle loves me, and when I die, and one of my own sister son will take my name, and when my sister son shall die also then this name will be back to Gishbouwawada, and when I die and my elder daughter bring some children, and she name her children to my relation relation name because she took my mother's name.

This is from a manuscript in the archives of the American Philosophical Society numbered Pn5a.2, which has heretofore been listed, by error, under William Beynon's name, see Freeman 1966:374, item 3776.

We also find Barbeau (1917:546) calling Tate a "half-breed," an "educated half-breed," which only complicates things further.

10 The completion of this present volume has been delayed year by year in hope that this crucial letter might turn up. But not only my own inquiries years ago but also Douglas Cole's more recent ones have been unavailing. I would like to pay tribute to my late colleague and friend by saying that if anyone could find this letter he could, and thus he releases this book into the public domain, with my thanks. It is a great loss that the companion volume to Douglas Cole's *Franz Boas: The Early Years, 1858-1906* (Vancouver: Douglas & MacIntyre; Seattle: University of Washington Press, 1999) will not now be written.

11 The Appendix A story about the Porcupine was written in February 1908, over two years after Boas tried to prevail on Tate to write the Tsimshian first.

12 Dell Hymes added: "This fact ought to be of interest to the growing number of students of literacy and its development in various cultural settings."

13 "I don't understand the Naas, for their language are different from us" Tate letter to Boas 29 May 1908 in Columbia University Library (abbreviated Columbia). Even the Nass words familiar to Tate would look strange in Boas's phonetic orthography.

14 When Boas chose the first few pages of the "Story of the Porcupine" as his sample of Tsimshian for the *Handbook of American Indian Languages* (Boas 1911:419-422), he omitted the "unintelligible" words without question marks or any comment at all.

15 When William Beynon rewrote this story for Boas from the printed text, he translated the song as "Dry up, dry up, really think too much of my children" (Ottawa: Barbeau Northwest Coast Files B-F- 148.3 p.198). He adds a note: "During the time of the North Winds, there comes the drying up by freezing of everything." Tate's "burn" should perhaps, then, be understood as drying not burning; but Beynon is not helpful in regard to the children.

16 The best conjecture is that Boas turned these two hundred or so pages over to someone for rechecking, and he did not get them back before his death. A letter from William Beynon to Philip Drucker of 8 March 1954 states: "I spent a few years in rewriting phonetically and re-translating for Dr. Boas, Tait's MSS. in fact I worked up to Dr. Boas's death and then I had to leave off, as the University (Columbia) was no longer interested in Tsimshian material" (letter in National Anthropological Archives, Smithsonian Institution, Drucker Collection #4516, part 50).

    Boas mentioned in a letter of 8 June 1934 to Viola Garfield that "during this last winter I have had Mr. Beynon rewrite for me the whole Tate materials which was written in such bad phonetics that I could not use it" (quoted in Halpin 1978:148). It would have taken more than a winter to do the whole of Tate. We do know that Beynon had pp.

1185-1716 of the Tate manuscripts, which are also missing from the Columbia collection. His rewritings are there, but the originals may have simply been discarded, thought to have been made redundant by his work—in keeping with general practice in regard to field notes at this time. Beynon's involvement does not really account for the missing originals of the stories in *Tsimshian Texts* (nor why the two Porcupine stories survived in manuscript, for that matter). We have documents that indicate he went over these stories, but clearly he was using the published volume. So where did these crucial Tate pages go? The hope of finding them has been another reason for delaying the publication of this present volume.

17 Reading thoughtlessly from the typist's version, Boas uses "Living Eyes" in his "Description of the Tsimshian" (1916:416) and in the summary of "The Deluge" on 1916:862. However, paraphrasing that story under the heading "Shamanism" (1916:473) he uses the correct "Living Ice."

18 In introducing this letter Stocking said, "In several cases where he came across a particularly capable informant, Boas taught him to record texts himself. Both George Hunt (son of a Scotsman and a Tlingit, who had grown up among the Kwakiutl) and Henry W. Tate (a full-blooded Tsimshian) in this way transmitted large bodies of material to Boas in New York" (Stocking 1989:85). We should set the record straight on a number of points. Boas's statement that Tate was "full-blooded" is by view of Barbeau's closer knowledge very much open to doubt (see footnote 9 above). Hunt's father was probably not Scottish but English. "Robert Hunt came to Victoria from Dorsetshire in the spring of 1850" (Healey 1958:19). I do not think it right to say that Boas "taught" Tate; but more than that, Stocking's unsuspecting approval of the Tate-Boas collaboration is something to be noted.

19 The transmission of the text here is doubly circuitous. Boas relied on Archie Dundas for the Tsimshian wording, as he had for the 1912 volume. But he saw the chance of an early publication in *Zeitschrift für Ethnologie*, so translated the Tsimshian into German (Boas 1908:776-797). When he was putting together the 1916 *Tsimshian Mythology* it was this German text that Boas translated into English; so we are further away from Tate's English than ever.

20 Garfield (1939:297) explains: "Because of restrictions placed on men's activities by the spirits, the season was called the 'time of tabu'." See also the footnote in the German edition (Boas 1908:794).

21 For convenience, I present the Columbia manuscript pp. 365-369 in the slightly edited form which I published in *The Porcupine Hunter and other Stories* (Maud 1993:123-125).

22 Halpin 1973:147-148. In spite of a promising title, "The Shining Youth in Tsimshian Mythology," an article by Brad C. Campbell (1975) pursues matters remote from our concerns.

23 William Beynon, Ottawa manuscripts #119 p. 2 notes. Beynon goes on to attest to Pierce's reliability: "He has always been a studious man, in fact studied for the ministry... He is much more intelligent than the average and in age is about 70 years."

24 David Ellis 1980, 1981. Ellis has informed me (personal communication) he has no information on whether or not Solomon Wilson might have had access to a copy of *Tsimshian Mythology*.

25 Halpin 1973:180. It was under the name of "Nees-yaranaet, head-chief of a Raven clan in the Gitsees tribe at Port Simpson" that Herbert Wallace gave to Beynon in 1926 a mythic description of his own totem pole—Barbeau 1950:348. For E. Maxwell, see Barbeau 1950: 248.

26 I am quoting here from the typescript, "A grammar of the Zimshian language, with some observations on the people" by Dr. William Ridley, Bishop of Caledonia, in the National Anthropological Archives, Smithsonian Institution (Ridley 1895).

27 Tate's adoptive father Arthur Wellington Clah talks about the "First People" under the heading "Tsimpsean Legends" in his "Reminiscences":

> There was a stone, about two, three, feet. There was a wild cherry tree. The stone had a son and the wild cherry tree had a son. The stone child came out too slow... If the stone child

> came first, people say they would never die. But cherry tree
> child came first, so people die all time.

This affirms the orthodoxy of Tate's version but it leaves out Raven as well as the shining youth.

28 Boas 1916:71. Here, as elsewhere, Tate's grammar degenerates somewhat when he leaves the script before him. Tate's words are: "he was wept. He said to the fish you looks like my grant-father, that was died little while ago He wipt off his tears from his eyes. He said, Come here ashore, or I will talk to you a while" (Columbia p. 418).

29 These were absorbed into the complete volume *Kwakiutl Texts* by Franz Boas and George Hunt, Vol. 3 of the Jesup Expedition, which was issued as Vol. 5 of the *Memoirs of the American Museum of Natural History* (Leiden 1905). Boas's initial letter to Arthur Wellington Clah of 15 April 1903 (AMNH) mentions he is sending, among the published volumes, "two of the Kwakiutl at Fort Rupert. The tales of the Kwakiutl were written down by George Hunt and by myself so we published jointly."

30 *Indianische Sagen* (1895), translation in typescript courtesy B.C. Indian Language Project 1977, "The Raven Legend" pp. 271-273, the informant identified on p. 273.

31 Dell Hymes *"In vain I tried to tell you"* (Philadelphia: University of Pennsylvania Press 1981); Dennis Tedlock *Finding the Center* (New York: The Dial Press 1972); Barre Toelken in ed. Karl Kroeber *Traditional Literatures of the American Indian* (Lincoln: University of Nebraska Press 1981). See Appendix C for an attempt to follow the Hymesian methodology in presenting the "Sucking Intestines" story as told by a master story-teller.

32 Manuscript (Columbia) by William Beynon titled "Tate's M.S.S. No. 15"—a retranscription and retranslation of the final pages of the "Gauo" manuscript pp. 38-42 plus one page of a song (Tate's pages themselves are to be found separated from the rest of the story, which is lost, in the Library of the American Philosophical Society). Beynon's rewriting corresponds to pp. 222-225 of *Tsimshian Texts* (1912), with more on

halait—i.e. Boas actually cut Tate off for publication. He could have cut him off a lot sooner.

33 This is an imprudent statement which can be easily refuted if one further example of Boas critical opinion is found. Someone might be provoked to search for another example and actually find it.

34 Psychological depths are apparently not something that Boas wanted to think about. Commenting on both Kwakiutl and Tsimshian myths of the son-in-law test type, he says, "My impression is that they are rather thought of as punishment for clandestine unions" (Boas 1935:174). Here is a father-in-law speaking.

35 John Asher Dunn's *Practical Dictionary of the Coast Tsimshian Language.* (1978) confirms this, giving ASDIWAAL as "to have an accident; to make a mistake.' (1978:7). Wilson Duff listed "As-de-wal" as the name of a Wolf Clan chief at Kitwancool; he had received the meaning "Accidentally" for the name (1959:43).

36 Although there seem to be no snowshoes nor any other mountain paraphernalia listed as crests of the Eagle clan, the chances are this is an Eagle crest story. Chief Mountain, an Eagle, told the story to Boas (1902:225-229). Emma Wright, an Eagle, told it to Beynon (MacDonald and Cove 1987: 170-171). Tate had been an Eagle before his adoption (Boas 1916:500). A later section of the story is in an Eagle crest myth in Barbeau's *Totem Poles* (1950:140-141), where Asdiwal's human wife is an Eagle Clan member.

37 We should note that Boas does not paraphrase very accurately. In this section, the concept of "when her husband as much as looks upon another woman" is not in the story: the plume is a test of adultery, simply that. Boas implies that Asdiwal just looked, but what he did was go to a "pretty young woman" who smiled at him at the drinking-place and "embrace" her. This *Tsimshian Texts* phrasing is no doubt itself a euphemism for what Tate actually wrote.

The Sun-Princess goes back up the sunbeam ladder to heaven; she does not walk across the ocean, as Boas has it. When Asdiwal sinks, it is not into water but back to the ground from a great height. Presumably

Boas's notes had the sun father-in-law's net, so Boas supposed, when he came to summarize from notes only, that there was water.

"His wife disappears and he returns to earth," says Boas. No, it's the reverse. They both return to the earth, then the wife disappears. These points may not be of great consequence singly, but they indicate a carelessness that is from time to time damaging, as we shall see.

38 A notable demonstration of the work involved in opening up the meaning and value of a classic body of traditional narratives is Robert Bringhurst's *A Story as Sharp as a Knife: The Classical Haida Mythtellers and Their World* (Bringhurst 1999).

39 Beynon microfilm A1416 (Ottawa B-F-148.2), notebook headed: "Tsimshian Material Beynon Vol. II November 1938." Beynon is redoing 1912:137 to the end of the story. There is a note: "continued from vol. I," but I have not been able to discover this vol. I. It is clear that Beynon is working from the printed *Tsimshian Texts* and not Tate's manuscripts. The notes are not so extensive nor illuminating as one might have expected.

40 Chief Mountain's version has a premonition of the ending when Asdiwal's father makes his first snowshoes and sends him into the mountains for bear. He doesn't see any bears: "Then his father demanded to see his snowshoes. He examined them and found that he had made a mistake in making them." (1902:226).

41 Following Lévi-Strauss's "The Story of Asdiwal" in *The Structural Study of Myth and Totemism*, edited by Edmund Leach (1967) pp. 1-47, is something of a rebuttal by Mary Douglas, pp. 49-69. "When Lévi-Strauss has finished with the Tsimshian myth," she says, "it is reduced to anxieties about problems of matrilateral cross-cousin marriage" (1967:63).

42 Referring to Boas's "Description of the Tsimshian, Based on Their Mythology," the distinguished contributors of the Tsimshian chapter in the Northwest Coast volume of the *Handbook of North American Indians* state: "While much of this work is convincing in the light of later work, insofar as it depends on myths it must be used with caution. Myths are not a reliable source on actual behavior" (Halpin and Seguin 1990:283).

Clearly, Boas thought they were: "They present in a way an autobiography of the tribe" (1916:393). Wayne Suttles has told me that he thinks Boas considered this "Description of the Tsimshian, Based on Their Mythology" and *Kwakiutl Culture As Reflected in Mythology* (1935) his proudest achievements.

43   T.F. McIlwraith was in Bella Coola for the Anthropological Division of the Canadian Geological Survey from March to August 1922 and from September 1923 to February 1924. His findings appeared in two volumes from the University of Toronto Press almost twenty-five years later. He had none of Boas's anxiety and rush, and his work competes with permanent resident ethnologists like Father Morice. *A Guide to B.C. Indian Myth and Legend* makes clear my bias toward local men who learned something from Boas but did not mesh with his machine. For instance, Charles Hill-Tout, living in Vancouver, went time after time to nearby Indian settlements and built up trust and friendship; see his collected papers, *The Salish People: the Local Contribution of Charles Hill-Tout* (Maud 1978). A lifetime in one locality gave Oliver Wells's *The Chilliwacks and Their Neighbours* (1987) an unbeatable authenticity and completeness.

44   Leslie Spier in his study of *Tsimshian Mythology* strikes a cautionary note: "Because of other non-folk-loristic evidence Boas chooses the alternative that the Tsimshian have come to the coast rather than that the tales have diffused from there and displaced coast forms" (1931:453). In the eons of time such traffic may have happened more than once.

45   Derek Freeman's *Margaret Mead and Samoa* (1983) was the first revelation to me that someone else had noticed serious cracks in the father's hauteur. Freeman's new book, *The Fateful Hoaxing of Margaret Mead* (1999) reveals—though Freeman does not put it quite this way— that it was Boas who did the hoaxing by encouraging Mead to think that a couple of young ladies could be speaking for the society as a whole.

Susanne Hilton and John Rath gave a large hint that all may not be well with Boas's Northwest Coast work in reviewing his definition of the Kwakwala word for the mythic cannibal; see Hilton 1982:59-64. Rath made more revelations in his 1992 contribution to the Salish Conference, in response to Judith Berman's paper the year before (Berman 1991). This latter piece, "The Production of the Boas-Hunt

Kwakwala Texts," is an indication that, in further work from Berman, Boas will receive the full, fair and expert evaluation that has been lacking for so long. See Berman 1997.

Appendices

Appendix A

The History of Porcupine
Adaoqum Aorita

7

While the time in the Fall when all the
1 Nunushga Ltha Kshecut ga a ltha
animals went into their Dens. Also the great
2 wan thant yequshka a gum gapt. Da wila
Grizzly Bear sat into his own Den for
3 di dhash ga wi Inideak ashga vidi gapt ga
Winter sleep, and the great rain descended
4 a ga wi Gaunushin, ada gunu wila gwanth
and therefore the drops of water in the great
5 washit gana lu lawal na gim gafuh ga
Grizzly Bear's den. and his fur is full
6 wi Inideak ga : ada ltha wila loguuh
of water and he was disappoint, as long as
7 gi liat, ada shim lu haka gaud. a shga
the rain. So he sat at the door of his
8 haga washit, mnu gum koha dhat a tha
Den looking out for some thing.
9 aga vi gapt. at mi ligi lip gauda gudint
And while he was there. Behold a Porcupine
10 ada ashi didhat a guet, Gushtana Aorita
coming along. as she passed the door of
11 gum yaat a guet. ashiet shga yaga lithau gut
great Grizzly Bear Den. That Grizzly
12 wi Inidek a hi gapt.   Da howga Inidek
Bear said. will you come in here
13 ___ ___ ga gina a giat. ___ ___
My friend. I will sup with you. Therefore

753

1 nichĕbunshgi midum ga kdtgil, nĭnĭ gun
the Porcupine turn in the great Grizzly

2 dawila gin a'outa ā awd wi midĕk gut
Bear. Den. Then the Grizzly Bear make

3 ā wˈgaft. Dat wila, we thiluksha wi—
a large fire. Then he caught the poor

4 midĕk gut, dat ᵗʰᵃ̂dukĭāgwa gushga lthgu
Porcupine. and bind her foot and hand.

5 A'outa, a dat ᵒ̣̇lk dadakltha gasheshiadlth ᵍᵃⁿᵒⁿ
and put her near the fire and burnt.

6 adat halth shgudida goga lukut ada gwaluka
her back fur with wildfire. Then the great

7 hagaut a lukut, hĭ adawila
Grizzly Bear have said to Porcupine. while

8 hou wi midĕk aohga lthgu a'outa ā
he was burnt her back fur. make frost

9 ltha gwalukga wˈlim hagawda. shik shuwan
your little unsightly animal. dwdwsih

10 nii lthgu shieta gu   du·du·uh
says the great Grizzly Bear. Yes. I will do

11 da·ya·ga wi midĕk a, dum walut
said the Porcupine. Master loose my kind

12 dayāga. A'outa shimogait lthu mun dddaklth ᵘᵉ
Then I will do what you want. but the great

13 Ada dum walu da ka hourut. yagai althga
Grizzly Bear won't hear. ᵏᵒ what the boor

14 nisha gau wi midĕk ā hourut. gu lthgu

751

rcupine said to him, Because he
1 A'outa
Rout   ash neat, Awil shim
was great and strong he has power
2 gul wi'liksh ada gutgiat, neata ga gutgiat
over all animals so he did not hear
3 a tkanu yeyirhk, shmi gun altkgut hanok
what poor Animal that is the Porcupine
4 gapa hou ltkgu A'outa — — — — `
have said to him. His front heart was
5 aks houit ash kut, Agakoha k gand ash
against her. Then he kick her into
6 keat, — — Dat gik la gou klthak did
the fire once more make frost you
7 gun w'lukut, shikshu'na — — —
little ugly Porcupine. du, du'nh, said
8 ltkgu shitdukuk — — du, du'nh, dayaga
the great Grizzly Bear. He mocked the poor
9 wi midek. At nishgutgwoh ga ltkgua
Porcupine. Then the back fur of Porcupine
10 A'outa Da gik haduk gwaluk w'tim ha-gau
burnt. (So all the porcupine back hot much
11 Routa. shmi guor wal n'ga hagau tkami
fur now.) Now when these poor weak
12 A'oula ga'on, wai ltha alashgu ltkgu gweak am
Animal almost dead. For the scorched
13 yeyirhk ltka dum gakt. Awil ltha dalbukga
her skin, she said to great Grizzly Bear. have

149

755.
Midek

1. ...u anashim hagau da housh gushga wi .
mercy on me sir I will do for what you
2. gumgaudena gwi shimoiginat ltha dum waluda
wanted. Then again the Grizzly Bear
3. Wi'howau. Dat gup gik lagou k. lthak wi
kicked her against the fire. said the
4. Midek a gum wi'lukut, a houit
same words Make a frost you little
5. a shiedi housh shikshwanii lothgu
unsightly animal. The great Grizzly
6. shitdukgu a. — Wi haldit gwila
Bear done it many times, and when
7. gut wi Midek. ada ltha dum
the poor thing was dying. He thrown
8. gak gweam gau gwai. Dat sha ksha
her out side his Den, there she layed
9. oit dida tha aka b'gaput, gumi guba wil
a long while. And when she opened
10. gaga shgu dit; ada ltha gaga k..gel
her eyes, and tried to walk away, with
11. did, ada wilat baldum ya'at a shim gul
pain all over her body. she began to
12. gwaska thaui thamau, Da wil gaba.
cry say. your big ugly great power
13. hou, nugum wi shgaguum gutgintum
Grizzly Bear, don't say anything if you
14. Midek. gilau ga huum a geda

frozen to dead in your Den. Then

1 lu tkul däöt gagun ā awan.   Da gaba
she walk away slowly. And she began

2 wila yä'at ā hagwil yä'at, ada wil Koha
to sing a song her moarning song

3 lthaaut amhoum llëmi a'at di wi houduka dit

As I was walk at the foot of a beautiful green leaves mountain
wil dip ya ga w'daupishga ga lakokeak dzi o.

Then the stars of heaven ure glittering as the skys all clear for south
wudit gun baut gulth walgulth w'yan gulth siälshtā

alter maaaunyth Kohaama
She repeated this four times with crying.

5 ni ltha tkaikk li ya'an. ā wi houit
at the end of four times. Then the north

6 ltha shaba tkalök houit. Da gwantk ovi
wind began to blew and all the stars it the

7 girkiiyeashk, — . —   ada tkani biäläsk ta Koha
sky was twinkles as the north wind signs

8 oudi a libiläpilt ā shen la'dukshun dum go
to blew hart. Then the north wind blew hart

9 girkiiashk.   Da wila gwantga bäshk
and it became very cold and every thing

10 ada shun gal gwatk. . — ada tkani aau
was frozen Now the great Grizzly Bear

11 dau Däöt whai gu wi madik
was also frozen to dead in his Den

12 ltha di wi lu tkul däötum gakt a wzim

757.

for he was mock with weak and
1 Awilt nishkat gut gish dida ga, lthgwa alashgudit dilth
smaller than himself. The great Grizzly
2 gwa ga goshk dorh al riat, Dali gauda wi
Bear thought to himself while he was
3 madik a lh ashi hiiagnt.
mocking to the weak and little poor
4 nishkat ksha lthgwa alashgugum gwa'am.
Porcupine that no one could take
5 Grouta, a althgut nelth dum trin
the poor Porcupine out from his hand
6 kpa ga ltha Grouta a gum anant.
But the North wind avenge the poor weak
7 Ya gai wi gishieash gut in duinth lthgu alashgu gum
animal for her foes.
8 yipishk a d in libalukoha.
(The history of Porcupine and Beaver)
9 Adavgum Grouta ada shaul shyaul
As the Porcupine was walking around
10 ashi li lu tgwa ya shga Grouta a riga
a great Lake one day. Also the Beaver
11 wi likshim Dhat a gull da shat. Daal di
are swimming on the great Lake to
12 gulth lu tgwa lthu wi shyaul a wi gum chat
enjoy herself and struck her side
13 a lthgushgu adat yepa ai wi
tail on the water and plunge often

Tsimshian Texts (New Series) (1912:236-241)

5. Ada'ᵘgam a'utaga.

Ninlı̄'sga ła ksı̄'utgaᵉ a ła wa'nsga txanlı̄'sga ya'tslɛs⸗
gɛsga na-ga-tslɛnı-tsla'ptgaᵉ. Da wula dı̄·tlẫᵉnga wi-mɛdı̄'ᵉk
gᴇsga ₙ ndi-tsla'pt a dza wi-gẫ'msɛmgaᵉ. Ada ga'ni-wula
ₖwa'ntgᴇsga wẫ'sgaᵉ, da g·ik lu-la²wa'l nɛ-tslɛm-tsla'psga
wi-mɛdı̄'ᵉkgaᵉ. Ada g·ik lǒ'gaks gᴇsga n-lı̄ᵉtgaᵉ. Ada
sᴇmgal lu-hẫᵉxgᴇsga gẫᵉt gᴇsga sga-na'ksga wẫᵉstgaᵉ.
Ninlı̄' gan ksᴇ-tlẫᵉt gᴇsga nᴇ-txa-a'gasga n-tsla'ptgaᵉ. At
nıᵉⁿ ligi-lɛp-gẫᵉ gᴇsga kᵘdōᵉntgaᵉ.

Ada ası̄ dᴇtlẫᵉt gᴇsga gwa'sga, gakstatnẫᵉga a'utaga
gun-hēᵉtgᴇt gᴇsga awẫᵉtgaᵉ. Ası̄t sga-yẫᵉt gᴇsga n-lᴇksẫ'⸗
gasgᴇ n-tsla'psgᴇ wi-mɛdı̄ᵉkgaᵉ, adaᵉ wul ha'usga wi-mᴇ-
dı̄ᵉkgaᵉ, "Tslı̄ᵉna g·ēᵉt, n-sı̄ᵉplᴇnsgī. Mᴇ dᴇn kla-xdı̄ᵉyut."
Ninlı̄' gan da' wula tslı̄ᵉnsga a'ut gᴇsga awẫᵉsga wi-
mᴇdı̄ᵉkgaᵉ.

Adẫᵉ wula wi-sᴇ-la'ksᴇsga wi-mɛdı̄ᵉkgaᵉ; adat sa-gẫᵉsga
łgu-a'utagaᵉ. Adat dᴇkda'klᴇsga ga-sᴇsı̄ᵉtgaᵉ dıł ga-an'ō'ntgaᵉ. Adat hał-sgᴇ'rᴇt gᴇsga dzǒ'gasga la'ktgaᵉ. Adat wul
gwa'lklᴇnsga haklẫᵉsga łgu-a'utga. Nı̄ adaᵉ wul ha'usga
wi-mᴇdı̄ᵉk asga łgu-a'ut gᴇsga ła gwa'lksga n-lı̄ᵉm ha-
klẫᵉt-gaᵉ. "(Siksū'an nıᵉ łgu-sı̄ᵉta gu)¹ duu," da-ya'ga
wi-mᴇdı̄ᵉkgaᵉ. "Dᴇm wẫ'lud," da-ya'ga a'utagaᵉ. "Sᴇm'ẫ'-
g·id, łūᵉn dᴇda'kłᴇt, ada dᴇm wul wẫ'lu da nᴇ-hẫ'unt."
Y'lagai-a'łgᴇt nᴇsegẫ'tga wi-mᴇdı̄ᵉkga ha'usgaᵉ łgu-a'uta
gas nıᵉtgaᵉ, a wul sᴇmgal wi-gatg·a'tgaᵉ. Nıᵉtga kła-
ɡatg·a'dᴇt gᴇsga txanlı̄ᵉsga ya'tslᴇskgaᵉ. Ninlı̄' gan-a'łgᴇt
nlᴇxnlū' kłabᴇ-hа'usga łgu-a'ut gᴇs nıᵉtgaᵉ. Sᴇmgal wi-

¹ O, Siksū'ana łgu-sitdukuk. The sentence is unintelligible.

ẫ'dzᴇksgaᵉ, adat g·ik lagauk-kła'xsᴇt gᴇsga tslᴇm-n-la'ktgaᵉ.
"(Siksū'ana) łgu-sitdukuk)¹ duu duu," da-ya'ga wi-mᴇdı̄'ᵉk
a'sgat nsga'tgᴇsga łgu-a'utagaᵉ. Ada g·ik ha'tslᴇksᴇm
gwa'lksga n-lı̄ᵉm haklẫᵉsga a'utgaᵉ. Ninlı̄' gana wẫl nᴇ-
ga-haklẫᵉ txanlı̄ᵉsga a'utgaᵉ g·a'wun.

Wẫi, ła ala'sgusgᴇ łgu-gwẫᵉm ya'tslᴇskgaᵉ adaᵉ ła dᴇm
dzakt, a wul da'lbᴇksga na-anẫ'sᴇm haklẫᵉtgaᵉ, ada
wul ha'ut gᴇsga wi-mᴇdı̄ᵉkgaᵉ, "G·am-gẫ'dᴇna kłẫ'i, sᴇm'ẫ'⸗
g·id, ła dᴇm wẫ'lu da n-ha'un," dat g·ap-g·ik lagauk-kłẫ'x⸗
sᴇtga wi-mᴇdı̄ᵉk gᴇsga tslᴇm-n-la'ktgaᵉ, asga ha'ut gᴇsga
sı̄ᵉ-di-ha'utgaᵉ, "(Siksū'ana łgu-sitdukuk)¹ duu duu."
Wi-hēᵉldᴇt wilẫ'gutga wi-mᴇdı̄ᵉkgaᵉ. Ada ła dᴇm dza'ks⸗
ga łgu-gwẫᵉm a'utaga dat wul sa-ksᴇ-ō'łt gᴇsga txa-a'xsga
n-tsla'ptgaᵉ. Ninlı̄' kłabᴇ-wul-na'ksga sgᴇ'rᴇtgaᵉ, adat ła
qlẫ'gasga n-tsla'łtgaᵉ. Adat wul bẫᵉłdᴇ dᴇm yẫᵉtgaᵉ,
sᴇmgal wẫ'mxgᴇtga txa-nlı̄ᵉsga txamẫᵉtgaᵉ. Da wul kłabᴇ-
ha'utgaᵉ, "N gan-wi-sa-dzẫ'gan wi-gatg·a'dᴇm mᴇdı̄'ᵉk.
G·ilẫ' dzᴇ ha'un a dzᴇ da ła lu-txal-dẫ'un a awẫ'ⁿ." Da
kłabᴇ-wula-hagul-yẫᵉtgaᵉ. Ada' wult ksᴇ-łẫᵉsga am-ha'um
lı̄ᵉmitgaᵉ. Ada wi-hẫ'utgᴇtgaᵉ,

"Wul g·íldᴇp-yẫ'iga dū'bᴇsga łᴇksẫᵉx (di-wudit gan-bᴇt kuł-wẫ'l kuł-n'yẫn)
kuł-biẫ'łsta ał magẫ'nł K-siẫ'na, ał magẫ'nł K-łō'ssm."²

Nı̄ ła txa'lpxsgat liẫᵉntgaᵉ a wi-hẫ'utgᴇtgaᵉ, ła saba'
txa'lpxasga ha'utga, da gwẫ'ntga wi-g·isi-ẫᵉskgaᵉ. Ada
txanlı̄' biẫ'łsta ksᴇ-ga'udit a łᴇpla'plᴇlt ẫ sᴇ-nlẫᵉdīksᴇ dᴇm
gatg·a'tgᴇ g·isi-ẫᵉskgaᵉ. Dẫᵉ wula gwẫ'ntga bẫᵉsk. Ada'
sᴇmgal gwa'tkgaᵉ. Ada' txanlı̄' gẫ'gᴇ dudẫ'utgaᵉ.

Wẫi, ninlı̄ᵉsgᴇ wi-mᴇdı̄ᵉkgaᵉ gu lu-txal-dẫ'ut gᴇsga n-
tsla'ptgaᵉ. Ada' dza'ktgaᵉ a wult nᴇsga'tgᴇsga łgu-ala'skᵘ⸗

¹ Unintelligible.

dᴇt dıł gwa-kłẫ-tslūᵉsgᴇdᴇs ałt nıᵉtgaᵉ. Ha-łli-gẫᵉtsga
wi-mᴇdı̄ᵉkgaᵉ ẫ asi hi-ẫᵉgut nᴇsga'tgᴇsga łgu-ala'sgum
gwẫᵉm a'utagaᵉ, ẫ a'łgᴇt nẫᵉł dᴇmt' łn-xbᴇ-gẫᵉsga łgu-a'uta
a tslᴇm-an'ō'ntgaᵉ. Y'lagai-wi-g·isi-ẫᵉsgᴇt' łn-dı̄ᵉntgᴇsga łgu-
ala'sgum ya'tslᴇskgaᵉ. Ada' ninlı̄'t' łn-lᴇbẫᵉlsᴇtgaᵉ.

---

5. Story of the Porcupine.

It was when it was fall, and all the animals were in
their towns. Then Great-Grizzly-Bear was also in his
town because it was mid-winter. Then rain came down
and dropped into the den [town] of Great-Grizzly-Bear,
whose fur was wet; and he was much annoyed on account
of the long rain. Therefore he sat outside of the door
of his den and looked about for something.

While he was sitting there, behold! Porcupine went
towards him. As he passed the door of Great-Grizzly-
Bear's den, Grizzly-Bear said, "Come in, friend! Come
in, friend! You shall eat with me." Therefore Porcupine
entered the den of Grizzly-Bear.

Then Great-Grizzly-Bear made a great fire. He took
little Porcupine, tied his feet and hands, and put him by
the side of the fire. Then Porcupine's back was burned
by the fire. Great-Grizzly-Bear said, "? ? ? du-u, du-u!"
Thus said Great-Grizzly-Bear. "I shall do so," said Porcupine. "O chief! untie my bands, then I will do what
you say."

But Great-Grizzly-Bear did not mind what little Porcupine said to him, because he is very strong. He is the
strongest among all the animals, therefore he did not
listen to what little Porcupine said to him. He was very
proud, therefore he kicked him again into the fireplace.
"? ? ? du-u, du-u!" said Great-Grizzly-Bear, making fun of
little Porcupine. Then the hair on the back of Porcupine
was burned again. Therefore the backs of all porcupines
are this way now.

When the poor weak little animal was about to die
because the skin of his back was shrivelled up, she said
again to Great-Grizzly-Bear, "Have pity on me, chief!
I will do what you say." But then Great-Grizzly-Bear
kicked him again into the fireplace, and said, what he had
said before, "? ? ? du-u, du-u!"

Great-Grizzly-Bear did so many times. When the poor
little Porcupine was about to die, he threw him out of his
den, and the poor one lay there for a long time. Then
he opened his eyes. He tried to walk, but his whole body
gave him much pain. Then the poor one said, "I have
reason to be ashamed of you, great strong Grizzly-Bear.
Don't say anything when the ice comes to you." Then
the poor one went along slowly. He went out, singing
a crying-song, and he cried,

"As I walk at the foot of a beautiful green mountain,
All the stars of heaven are glittering as the north wind clears the sky."²

When he had repeated his cry four times, and when
he had finished saying it the fourth time, the wind began
to blow down river. Then all the stars came out and
twinkled, and indicated that there would be a strong wind
down river. Then the wind came, and was very cold,
and everything was ice.

It was Great-Grizzly-Bear who was caught by the ice
in his den. Then he was dead, because he had made

² The translation of the song is not clear. So far as the words are intelligible,
they may be translated as follows: "Around the foot of the door goes ? ? ? Fog
is around, stars are around the head waters of the Skeena River and the head waters
of Nass River." The translation given above is the interpretation of the song given
by Mr. Tate.

fun of the poor weak one, who was smaller than he.
It was the wish of Great-Grizzly-Bear when he began to
make fun of the poor weak little Porcupine, and there
was nobody who took away poor Porcupine from his hands.
Nevertheless the strong wind down river avenged the
poor weak animal. He was the one who hated him.

Appendix B

The *Tsimshian Texts* version of the origin of Raven (1902:7-10)

Txä′msem and LôG̣ôbolā′

[1-5 told by Moses; 6-8, 2a and 5a told by Philip]

1. There was a town in which a chief and chieftainess were living. The chieftainess had done something bad. She had a lover, but the chief did not know it. The young man loved the chieftainess very much. He often went to the place where she lived with the chief. Then the chieftainess resolved, "I will pretend to die." She pretended to be very sick, because she wanted to marry that man. After a short time she pretended to die. Then all the people cried. Before she died the chieftainess said, "Make a large box in which to bury me when I am dead." The people made a box and put her

---

Txä′msem and LôG̣ôbolā′

1. Hētkᵘʟ qal-ts’a′p. Nʟk·’ē k·’âlʟ sɛm’â′g·it dē-k·’âlʟ sîg·idɛmna′q.   1
There stood   a town.   Then   one   chief   and one   chieftainess.

Nʟk·’ē sg·īʟ hwîlʟ sîg·idɛmna′q. K·’âlʟ ʟgo-g·a′tg·ê, nʟnē t’an   2
Then   had   done   the chieftainess.   One   little   man,   he   who
  something

lēlē′luksʟ sîg·idɛmna′q. Nî′g·ît hwîlā′x·ʟ sɛm’â′g·it. Sɛm-sī′epɛnʟ   3
stole often   the chieftain-   Not   knew it   the chief.   Very   he loved
  ess.

sîg·idɛmna′q t’an qaqâ′ôdet aʟ dɛd’ā′t aʟ awa′aʟ sɛm’â′g·it. Nʟk·’ē   4
the chieftainess   who   went there   to   she was   in proximity   the chief.   Then
  often   of

tgōnʟ sa-gâ′ôtkᵘʟ sîg·idɛmna′q: "Āmʟ dɛm nô′ôēe aʟ dɛm   5
this   resolved   the chieftainess: "Good   (fut.)   I am   and   (fut.)
  dead

sī-bē′ɛkᵘsēe." Nʟk·’ē ā′d’îkskᵘʟ dɛm hwîl sī′epkᵘʟ sîg·idɛmna′q.   6
make   I lie."   Then   came   (fut.)   being   sick   the chieftainess.

Nʟk·’ē wī-t’ē′sʟ ha-sī′epkᵘʟ aʟ sī-bē′kᵘstg·ê dɛmt hwîla nak·skᵘʟ   7
Then   was great   sickness   at   she   a lie   (fut.)   trying   she wanted
  made   to marry

k·’âlʟ g·at, qan hēt. Nîg·i nakᵘʟ sg·ēʟ sîg·idɛmna′q, nlk·’ē   8
one   man,   there-   she   Not   long   lay   the chieftainess,   then
  fore   said so.

nô′ôt. Nʟk·’ē sig·a′tkᵘʟ txanē′tkᵘʟ qal-ts’a′p. Nʟk·’ē tgōnʟ hēʟ   9
she was   Then   cried   all the   people.   Then   this   said
dead.

sîg·idɛmna′q: "Tsɛ sī-laîsɛm xpêîs tsɛ hwîl lō-sg·i′eɛ." ʟa nô′ôt, 10
the chieftainess: "Make   that large   a box   where in   I shall   When she was
  lie."   dead,

nlk·’ēt dzā′pdēʟ xpêîst. Nʟk·’ēt lō-ma′qdēt lâ′ôt. Nʟk·’ēt 11
then   they made   a box.   Then   in   they put   in it.   Then
  her

7

into it. They put it on the branches of a tree in the woods. The chieftainess had a spoon and a fish knife in her box. She pretended to be dead. For two nights the chief went into the woods, and sat right under the box in which the chieftainess was lying. Then he ceased to cry. Behold, there were maggots falling down from the bottom of the box. Then the chief thought, "She is full of maggots." But actually the chieftainess was scraping the spoon with her fish knife, and the scrapings looked just like maggots. In the evening her lover went into the woods. He climbed the tree and knocked on the box, saying, "Let me in, ghost!" He said so twice. Then the chieftainess replied, "Ha-ha! I pretend to make maggots out of myself

1 q'aldîx·-ma'qdet   aL   g·îlē'lîx·.   Nᴌk·''et   ma'qsaandēᴌ   gan.
in the rear   they put   at   in the woods.   Then   they put her on   a tree.
of the houses   her

2 Ts'ō'sg·îm   nakᵘ,   nᴌk·''ēt   lō-dā'mᴌ   sîg·idᴇmna'qᴌ   q'aldō'x·   qanᴌ
A little   while,   then   in   held in   the chieftainess   a spoon   and
                            her hands

3 ha-q'ō'ᴌ.   Bēkᵘᴌ   hwî'ltg·ê.   Nîg·idē   nô'ôt.   Nᴌa   g·ē'lp'ᴇl   yu'ksa
a knife to   She lied   she did so.   Not she   was   (Perf.)   two   evenings
split salmon.   dead.

4 qa'nē-hwîla   q'aldîx·-iä'ᴌ   sᴇm'â'g·ît   aᴌ   lôgôl-dᴇp-d'ā't   aᴌ   ᴌaXᴌ
always   to the rear went   the chief   under   he sat   at   under
       of the houses

5 hwîl   lē-sg·īᴌ   xpē'îs   hwîl   lō-sg·īᴌ   sîg·idᴇmna'q.   ᴌa   ᴌēskᵘᴌ
where   on   was   the box   where   in   lay   the chieftain-   When   finished
                                ess.

6 wi-yē'tkᵘᴌ   sᴇm'â'g·ît,   gwinā'dēᴌ,   smā'wun   qa'nē-hwîla   mak·t   aᴌ
crying   the chief,   behold,   maggots   always   fell   at
                                       down

7 bakᵘt   aᴌ   siä'nᴌ   xpē'îst.   Nᴌk·''ē   tgōnᴌ   hēᴌ   qâtᴌ   sᴇm'â'g·ît:
came   at   the bottom   the box.   Then   this   said   the heart   the chief:
out of   of   of

8 "ᴌa   smā'wun   da."   Dē'yaᴌ   qâ'ôtᴌ   sᴇm'â'g·ît.   Tgōnᴌ   hwîlᴌ
"It is all maggots."   Thus said   the heart   the chief.   This   did
                       of

9 sîg·idᴇmna'qg·ê.   ᴌa'lbᴇᴌ   q'aldō'x·   aᴌ   ha-q'ō'ᴌ.   Nᴌk·''ēt   hō'g·îgaᴌ
the chieftainess.   She   the spoon   with   the fish   Then   like
               scraped   knife.

10 smā'wunᴌ   ᴌä   q'am-ᴌä'lbᴇqskt   aᴌ   q'aldō'x·.   Nᴌk·''ē   huX   yu'ksa.
maggots   (perf.)   refuse of   scraping   at   the spoon.   Then   again   it was
                                           evening.

11 Nᴌk·''ē   huX   q'aldîx·-iä'ᴌ   an-k'ō'oXt.   Nᴌk·''ēt   mᴇn-hē't'ᴇnᴌ   gan.
Then   again   to the rear went   her sweetheart.   Then   up   he placed   a tree.
              of the houses

12 Nᴌk·''ē   mᴇn-iä'ᴌ   g·a'tg·ê.   Nᴌk·''ēt   nä-d'îsd'ē'st.   Nᴌk·''ē   tgōnᴌ
Then   up   went   the man.   Then   with   he   Then   this
                            his hand knocked.

13 hē'tg·ê: "Ts'ēnt'ᴇnē,   lū'laq.   Ts'ē'ntᴇnē,   lū'laq." [1]   G·'ē'lp'ᴇlᴌ
he said: "Let me   ghost.   Let me   ghost."   Twice
         enter,   enter,

14 hē'tg·ê.   Nᴌk·''ē   dē'lᴇmᴇxkᵘᴌ   sîg·idᴇmna'q: "Hǎhä,   algwâ'ᴌ
he said so.   Then   answered   the chieftain-   "Hǎhä,   therefore
                                  ess:

15 qan   sîsqaxsä'ntg·ê."   Nᴌk·''ēt   hux   q'angō'uᴌ   ᴌa   hä'bᴇᴌ   an-sg·ē'îst.
I pretend to make mag-   Then   again   she opened   the cover   the grave.
gots out of myself."   of

---

[1] These words are in Tsimshian dialect.

in your behalf." Then she opened the cover of the box, and the man
lay down with her. He did so every night. Then she came to be
pregnant. The man always went up to her. The chief did not know
it, but one man found it out. He told the chief. Then the chief's
nephews kept watch and killed the man, and also killed the woman.
Now she was really dead, and her body was putrefying. Then her
child came out alive. It sucked the intestines of its mother, and therefore its name was Sucking-intestines. The child grew up in the box.

One day all the children went into the woods, shooting with bows
and arrows at a target. They were not far from this tree when they
were shooting. Then Sucking-intestines saw them. He went down
and took their arrows. Thus the children lost them again and again.

Nᴸk·'ē huX lō-g·ä'êʟ g·at aʟ awa'at. Txanē'tkᵘʟ axkᵘʟ hwîlt. 1
Then again in lay the in her prox- Every night he did so.
down man imity.

Nᴸk·'e ʟa ä'd'îk·skᵘʟ dᴇm ō'bᴇnt. Nᴸk·'ē ō'bᴇnt qa'nē-hwîla 2
Then (perf.) she came (fut.) pregnant. Then she was always
pregnant

bax-iä'ʟ g·a'tg·ê. Nî'g·it hwîlä'x·ʟ sᴇm'â'g·ît. Hwä'i! K·'âlʟ 3
up went the man. Not knew it the Well! One
chief.

g·a'tg·ê t'an lō-hwa't. Nᴸk·'ēt ma'ʟdet aʟ sᴇm'â'g·ît. Nᴸk·'ēt 4
man who in found Then he told to the chief. Then
it.

lēʟʜ ʟ guslî'skᵘʟ sᴇm'â'g·ît. Nᴸk·'ēt dza'kᵘdēʟ g·a'tg·ê. Nᴸk·'ē 5
watched the nephews the chief. Then they killed the man. Then
of

huX dza'kᵘdēʟ hana'qg·ê. Nᴸk·'ē sᴇm-hō'm nô'ôt. Hwä'i! ʟa 6
also they killed woman. Then really she Well! (Perf.)
the was dead.

lôqʟ lō'ʟᴇqg·ê. Nᴸk·'ē k·saxʟ ʟgo-tk·'ē'ʟkᵘʟ dᴇdē'lstg·ê. Nᴸk·'ē 7
putrefy- her body. Then out came a little child alive. Then
ing was

d'âqʟ ʟgo-tk·'ē'ʟkᵘʟ hâts nôxt. Nʟʀêʟ qan hwa'dᴇs Anmâgôm 8
it sucked the child the in- of his Therefore its name Sucking-
little testines mother.

hä't. Hwäi! ʟa wī-t'ē'sʟ ʟgo-tk·'ē'ʟkᵘg·ê aʟ lō-d'ä't aʟ 9
intes- Well! When great was the child at in was in
tines. little

ts'ᴇm-xpē'îst. 10
in the box.

Nᴸk·'ē q'aldîx·-qâ'ôdᴇʟ txanē'tkᵘʟ k'ōpe-tk·'ē'ʟkᵘ wī-hē'lt 11
Then to the rear of they were all the little children many
the houses gone

yukʟ sg·äela'xkᵘdētg·ê aʟ ha-Xda'kʟ dô'qdēt qanʟ hawî'l. 12
while they shot at a with bows they took and arrows.
target

Wagait-dō' hwîl hētkᵘʟ gan. Nʟnēʟ gu'Xdēit. Nᴸk·'ē g·ig·a'as 13
At a distance far where stood a tree. Then they shot. Then saw
them

Anmâgôm hä't. Nᴸk·'ē huX d'ᴇp-ie'êt. Nᴸk·'ēt huX dôqʟ 14
Sucking- intes- Then again down he Then again he took
tines.

ha-wî'l. Nᴸk·'ē huX k'ut-gwâ'disîʟ txanē'tkᵘʟ k'ōpᴇ-tk·'ē'ʟkᵘ. 15
arrows. Then again about lost them all the little children.

Now, the children saw that the boy came from out of the grave, and they told the chief. He said, "Keep watch and try to catch him." The chief's nephews went, and, behold, he came down again. While he was walking about, they caught him and took him home. They took him to the chief's house. Now he grew up, and his name was Sucking-intestines.

2. Now he heard that there was a chief's daughter on the other side of the hole where the heavens meet. Sucking-intestines caught a bird and skinned it. He put its skin on and flew. Then he said, "G·ît g·ît g·ît g·însääää!" He came to a town, and there he met a person. Then he shot a wood-pecker. He skinned it, and the other person put it on. They flew on. The one bird cried, "G·ît g·ît g·ît g·însääää!" The wood-

---

1 Nʟk·'ē   ʟā   sī-gō'n,   nʟk·'ē   hwîlā'x·detg·ê   hwîl   g·ik·si-hwî'tkᵘʟ
  Then   when a little   then   they knew   where out   came from
            while,

2 ʟgō-tk·'ē'ʟkᵘ   aʟ   ts'ɛm-an-sg·ē'îst.   Nʟk·'ēt   ma'ʟdēit   aʟ   sɛm'â'g·ît.
  the boy from   in   the grave.   Then   they   to   the chief.
  little   told

3 Nʟk·'ē   a'lg·îxʟ   sɛm'â'g·ît: "Ām   mɛsɛm   lēʟk·t   sɛm-g·idi-gō'uʟ."
  Then   spoke   the chief: "Good you   watch   very right take him."
                                                                 there

4 Nʟk·'ē   hwîlʟ   guslî'skᵘʟ   sɛm'â'g·ît.   Gwinādē'ʟ,   ʟa   huX
  Then   they did so the nephews the chief.   Behold,   when again
                        of

5 d'ɛp-ā'd'îk·skᵘt,   nʟk·'ē   huX   k'uʟ-iä'êt.   Nʟk·'ē   sā-t-gō'udet.
  down   he came,   then   again about he went. Then   sud-   they took
                                                               denly   him.

6 Nʟk·'ēt   na-dē-iä'edet.   Nʟk·'ē   ts'ɛlɛm-ma'qdet   aʟ   awa'aʟ
  Then   out of with they Then   into   they   at   the prox-
            woods him went.   put him   imity of

7 sɛm'â'g·ît.   Nʟk·'ē   wī-t'ē'st,   Anmâgôm   hā'ʟ   hwa'tg·ê.
  the chief.   Then   he was large, Sucking-   intes- was his name.
                                                   tines

8 2.   Nʟk·'ēt   nɛxna'ʟ   hwîl   d'āʟ   ʟgō'uʟkᵘʟ   sɛm'â'g·ît   aʟ   an-dâ'ʟ
       Then   he heard   where was   the daughter of a chief   at   other side
                                                                          of

9 hwîl   nanô'ôʟ   mɛsmā'ʟ   lax-ha'.   Nʟk·'ēt   gō'us   Anmâgôm   hā'ʟ
  where the hole of the meeting the sky.   Then he   took   Sucking-   intes-
                      of   tines

10 g·îtg·însa'.   Nʟk·'ēt   tsa'adēt.   Nʟk·'ēt   lō-ʟô'otkᵘt.   Nʟk·'ē
   (a bird).   Then   he skinned   Then   in he put it on. Then
                           it.

11 g·ebā'yukt.   Nʟk·'ē   a'lg·îxt: "G·ît   g·ît   g·ît   g·însääää."   Nʟk·'ēt
   he flew.   Then   he   "G·ît   g·ît   g·ît   g·însääää."   Then
                         said:

12 hwaʟ   k·'ēlʟ   qal-ts'a'p.   Nʟk·'ēt   gōʟ   k·'âlʟ   g·at.   Nʟk·'ēt
   he   one   town.   Then   he met one   person. Then
   found

13 gu'Xdēʟ   hā'atkᵘ.   Nʟk·'ēt   tsa'adetg·ê.   Nʟk·'ēt   lō-ʟô'ôtkᵘʟ
   he shot   a wood-   Then he   skinned it.   Then   in he put it on
             pecker.

14 k·'âlʟ   g·at.   Nʟk·'ē   lēba'yukdet.   Nʟk·'ē   huX   a'lg·îxʟ   g·îtg·însa':
   one   person. Then   they flew.   Then   again spoke   G·îtg·insa':

15 "G·ît   g·ît   g·ît   g·însääää."   Nʟk·'ē   dē-g·ebā'yukʟ   ha'atkᵘ:
   "G·ît   g·ît   g·ît   g·însääää."   Then   with   flew   the wood-
                                                                 pecker:

Appendix C: "The Birth of Greedy-One"

On 2 October 1894 Franz Boas embarked from Victoria for his fifth field trip up the coast of British Columbia. "The Boskowitz," he writes to his wife, "is still as uncomfortable as she was before. The beds are so short that one cannot even stretch out; the deck is so full of cargo that there is no place to even turn around" (Rohner 1969:148). But there are Natives on board, and they have promised to tell him stories. "Maybe I can get a few of their legends in their own language," he writes. "That would be really something" (1969:148). In a protracted four-day passage, Boas obtained what became the best fifty-eight pages of *Kwakiutl Tales* (Boas 1910). The informant is not named in the letters (Rohner 1969:150), but he left the ship at Nahwitti and was therefore almost certainly the Qomgilis, to whom these pages of *Kwakiutl Tales* are attributed (1910:208). Boas's field notebook of Qomgilis' stories is dated "Oct. 3," the first day out. Boas's confinement to shipboard guaranteed an uninterrupted concentration that was rarely allowed him on land—or so the extraordinary calibre of these narratives seems to prove.

The purpose of this appendix is to give a flavour of what a well-told story would be like in keeping with our investigation of the birth of Raven theme. I have attempted to follow the guidelines as given by Dell Hymes in *"In vain I tried to tell you"* (1981). Even a non-linguist can discern the pattern of "initial particles as markers of verse" (Hymes 1981:152); these markers have determined the layout of the text on the page. For comparison, Boas's presentation of the originally dictated text is added from *Kwakiutl Tales* (Boas 1910:208). My English narrative verse is taken from Boas's translation (1910:209).

The Birth of Greedy-One

Lalae   A woman was dead,
       the sweetheart of a man.
           Omaalaxol   Behold! she only planned
                        with her sweetheart
                        that the woman should
                        pretend to be dead.
Lalae   Then she was in the box,
       and she was taken into the woods.
Lalae   Then her sweetheart followed her,

and cohabited with her in the coffin.

<u>Omaalaxol</u>   Behold! the woman only
pretended to be dead,

<u>Lalae</u>   and she cohabited again with her lover.

<u>Lalae</u>   Then a slave of the chief
discovered (them).

"Why does this man go to your dead wife?"
said the slave to his master.

"Let us go: and see."
said the chief to his slave.

<u>Lalae</u>   Then they went and opened
the grave-box of his dead wife.

<u>Lalae</u>   She shut her eyes,

<u>Omaalaxol</u>   but behold! she was only lying.

<u>Lalae</u>   Then he took his knife,
and he cut open his dead wife.

<u>Laem</u>   Then his wife was really dead.

<u>Lemaalaxol</u>   Behold! she was pregnant.

<u>Lalae</u>   Then he took her child
and put it back into the box.

<u>Lalae</u>   He left it.

<u>Lalaaxaa</u> Then that slave again
discovered the child.

<u>Laemlae</u> The one who was cut out of
the dead wife was alive.

<u>Lalae</u>   Then he told his master.

"What have I seen?"
said the slave to his master.

"What is that child, if it is (not)
the one who was obtained
by being cut out of your dead wife?"
Thus said the slave.

<u>Lalae</u>   Then they looked.
what should there be
sitting in the box!

<u>Lalae</u>   Then he took it up in his arms
and took it out of the woods to his house.

(Dictated by Q!ō′mg·ilis, a ᵉnaqE′mg·ilisala, 1894.)

The Birth of Greedy-One.

Lā′ᵉlaē łEᵉlE′l yîxē ts!Edā′x. Wā′ḷadᵉlaē yîsē bEgwā′nEm. Ō̆ᵉmaāᵉlaxōḷ k!wē′xᵉîda ḷEᵉwis wā′ḷEla qaᵉs łEᵉlbō′łē yîxē′ ts!Edā′x. Lā′ᵉ|aē g·ī′ts!ō̆ᵉyâ lā′xē g·ī′ldas qaᵉs lē ā′ḷēᵉstayâ lā′xē ā′ḷ.!ē. Lā′ᵉlaē wā′ḷElaᵉyas lā′sgEmaq qaᵉs lē qaχ-ᵉwī′dax lā′xēs g·ī′ts!ō̆ᵉâs. Ō̆′ᵉmaāᵉlaxōḷ łEᵉlbō′ła yî′xē ts!E-dā′x. Lā′ᵉlaē ē′t!ēd qaxᵉwī′da lā′xēs wā′ḷEla. Lā′ᵉlaē dō′xᵉwaLEla yîx q!ā′k·âs yî′sē g·ī′gamaᵉē. "ᵉmā′tsai lā′xla-k·asᵉâs yîsē bEgwā′nEm lā′xēs gEnE′mx·daâs!" ᵉnē′x·ᵉlaēda q!ā′k·ō lā′xēs q!ā′gwidē. "Wai′x·înts dō′xᵉwīdqē," ᵉnē′x·-ᵉlaēda g·ī′gamaᵉē, lā′xēs q!ā′k·ō. Lā′ᵉlaē qā′sᵉîd qaᵉs x·ā′ux·ᵉîdēx lāx g·ī′ts!âsas yîsē′s gEnE′mx·dē. Lā′ᵉlaē k·!îxE′mx·ᵉîda. Ō̆′ᵉmaāᵉlaxōḷ q!ē′q!êk!wāla. Lā′ᵉlaē ax-ᵉē′dxē k·!ā′wayū qaᵉs qwā′xᵉîdēx lā′xēs gEnE′mx·dē. LaE′m â′lax·ᵉîda łEᵉla′ yîx gEnE′mx·das. LEᵉmaā′ᵉlaxōḷ bowē′χ-ᵉwīda. Lā′ᵉlaē axᵉē′da lā′xē g·inā′nEm qaᵉs k!wā′ts!ōdē χwē′laqas lā′xē g·ī′ldas. Lā′ᵉlaē bâ′las.

Lā′ᵉlaaxaa dō′xᵉwaLEla yîx q!ā′k·ōs lā′xē g·înā′nEm; laE′mᵉlaē q!u′la yîx qwā′ganEmas lā′xēs gEnE′mx·dē. Lā′ᵉlaē ᵉnē′ᵉlāla lā′xēs q!ā′gwidēx·: "ᵉmā′.dzē dō′gulân?" ᵉnē′x·ᵉlaēda q!ā′k·ō lā′xēs q!ā′gwidē. "ᵉmā′dzēda g·inā′nEm qao hë′Em-laxō, yîxē′s qwā′gānEmwułaōs lā′xēs gEnE′mwułaōs;" ᵉnē′x·-ᵉlaēda q!ā′k·ō. Lā′ᵉlaē dō′χᵉwid. ᵉmā′sLēᵉlaē k!wā′ts!âya lā′xē g·ī′ldas. Lā′ᵉlaē q!ałᵉē′dEx qaᵉs lē laō′łt!as lā′xēs g·ōχᵘ.

Appendix D: George Hunt's Asdiwal

A letter of 20 October 1916 is perhaps the only occasion on which Boas challenged the authenticity of any of George Hunt's work in mythology. He is returning a story "found among old papers" in order to give Hunt a chance to satisfy him on certain points:

> Would you kindly tell me where you collected it and what tribe the north-side tribe is; also if you have the Indian names of the people, like Pretty-Hunter on p. 18 and others, please send them to me. I know the story very well. It is really a Tsimshian story, but of course it may be that the Kwakiutl tell it too. (APS)

The request that Hunt name his source is not so innocent as it sounds. The item in question is a version, in English, of the well-known Asdiwal story, which Boas had just given great prominence to in the comparative sections of *Tsimshian Mythology* (Boas 1916: 792-825), combing the whole corpus of Northwest narratives for the remotest of analogues. If he had considered Hunt's story a genuine Kwakiutl version, he could not have done other than give it some attention in the discussion; but in fact it was left aside until *Tsimshian Mythology* was finished, and then casually questioned in the above letter.

The surprise is that when Hunt's reply comes in, dated 12 November 1916, he is emphatic that the story belongs to the Kwakiutl:

> This story was told by a kwekwEsote!nox man whose name was ts!oxts!aes. He had a uncle whose name was yaklEnleds the head chief of the brother tribe naxnoxula of the kwekwEsote!nox tribe. Now this chief wife was take slave by the BellxwEla tribe and she was sold to the northern tribes, and she stay up there for a long time, then she came home again. Now she might have told this story to her people. But ts!oxts!aes told me that this

story belong to his tribe and it is the pride of them. Will I translate it into kwagul or not. (APS)

The extant correspondence does not appear to include a copy of Boas's
rejoinder; but presumably Hunt was asked to return the story with
emendations (though not to translate it), and thus it is printed, in English
only, among the family histories of *Ethnology of the Kwakiutl* (Boas 1921:
1249-1255), with a full complement of Kwakiutl place-names and personal
names, and entitled, as per George Hunt's letter, "Legend of the Naxnaxu^{e}la,
Qweq^{u}sot!enox^u," but with no explanation of the provenance of the piece
nor its significance in terms of the Asdiwal theme.

Boas was satisfied to let the matter rest there until 1935 and *Kwakiutl
Culture as Reflected in Mythology*, when he referred to it in demonstrating
certain differences between the Tsimshian and the Kwakiutl:

> The difficulties of obtaining an adequate food supply must have
> been much more serious among the Tsimshian than among the
> Kwakiutl, for starvation and the rescue of the tribe by the deeds
> of a great hunter or by supernatural help are an ever-recurring
> theme which, among the Kwakiutl, is rather rare. One story of
> this type is clearly a Tsimshian story retold (R1249).
> (Boas 1935: 173).

R1249 is the page reference for our story in *Ethnology of the Kwakiutl*,
and the implication is that George Hunt's Asdiwal is not genuinely Kwakiutl.
(If the Asdiwal starvation theme were Kwakiutl as well as Tsimshian, that
would undermine the point Boas wants to make.) In repudiating the story as
Kwakiutl, however, Boas is negating Hunt's informant, Ts!oxts!aes, who was
insistent that the story belonged to his tribe. No matter that it may have
come with his uncle's wife from "the northern tribes," it was now felt not
only to "belong" to the Kwakiutl tribe but to be "the pride of them." How
can Boas ignore this? How can he ignore the title he gave the story when he
printed it in *Ethnology of the Kwakiutl?* The answer is that he can do so if
there is some overriding factor previously unstated. He can do so if he knows
that, whatever Ts!oxts!aes may or may not have said, the story in the form he

received it is literally a Tsimshian story retold, indeed, a rewriting by Hunt of Chief Mountain's version as published in *Tsimshian Texts* (Boas 1902: 225-229).

Tsimshian Texts (1902) was available to Hunt. It is included in his list of "texts of Books on Hand." That Hunt utilized Chief Mountain's "Asi-hwi'l" is a conclusion derived from elementary detective work. In the following sample, Chief Mountain's sentences have been numbered for ease of comparison with the corresponding segment of Hunt. Nothing has been omitted except the Native language words of the song in each case, as indicated.

Chief Mountain, *Tsimshian Texts* (Boas 1902: 227-228)

(1) A supernatural being who lives in heaven saw that Asi-hwi'l was a great hunter. (2) He covered one of his slaves with ashes, so that he looked like a white bear, and sent him to Nass River. (3) The hunters set out to kill the bear, but they were unable to reach it. (4) When the bear came to G'itxade'n, Asi-hwi'l put on his snowshoes, took his bag and his pole and pursued it. (5) The bear reached Leading Point. (6) There a vertical cliff rises, and the tracks of Asi-hwi'l's snowshoes where he climbed the cliff are still visible. (7) Beyond the cliff he saw the bear entering a large house. (8) He stayed at the door and heard the people singing: [music and Nishga words given]. (9) That is, "Asi-hwi'l is picking the bones of my neck." (10) Asi-hwi'l was unable to enter, and returned. (11) He had lost the bear.

George Hunt, *Ethnology of the Kwakiutl* (Boas 1921: 1252-1253)

(1) A supernatural being in heaven saw that Ex'sokwiᵉlakᵘ was a great hunter. (2) The supernatural being tried to capture the hunter: therefore he called one of his slaves and threw ashes over him. Then the slave was transformed into a grizzly bear. His master sent him up the river of Xekwek'En. (3) (4) When he was-going up, he came out on the beach near the house of Ex'sokwiᵉlakᵘ, because he wanted to be seen by the great hunter. As soon as Ex'sokwiᵉlakᵘ saw the bear, he gave chase. The bear went up a steep mountain, and the hunter put on his snowshoes, took his dogs and his long pole, and ran after him. (5) The bear climbed up to a point called Frog Point

(Wuxetbe^e). (6) There is a very steep and slippery cliff without a footing. (7) Nevertheless the hunter passed the dangerous place, and saw the great bear ahead of him going into a large house. (8) Then the hunter went to the outside of the house and listened. He heard many people singing inside. (9) They sang: "Prettiest-Hunter is picking the bone of my neck. [Kwakwala words given.] (10) He could not enter the house, and had to go home. (11) He lost the bear...

From such verbal closeness, common sense draws its obvious conclusion. Furthermore, just as the sentences or small units are co-extensive, so are the major episodes in these two versions. The fact that the hero does not enter the house is a significant case in point. In the other two Tsimshian versions, the *Indianische Sagen* (Boas 1895) and Tate's *Tsimshian Texts* (Boas 1912), Asdiwal does enter the house, marries the chief's daughter, and undergoes the son-in-law tests, all of this absent from Chief Mountain and Hunt. There are some differences between Hunt and Chief Mountain: Hunt is not uninventive; and his last section draws on a typically Kwakiutl revenge theme, where wealth triumphs. But all in all, one cannot help agreeing with what Boas said in his original letter of 20 October 1916, that Hunt's is "really a Tsimshian story." It is, indeed, as Boas must have known from the start, a particular published Tsimshian story.

Is it possible to think, by any stretch of the imagination, that Ts!oxts!aes got it from his ex-slave aunt in the form Hunt sent it to Boas? This is where old-fashioned literary criticism comes to the fore. We do have a narrative attributed to Ts!oxts!aes in *Kwakiutl Texts* (Boas 1905: 165-247). It is one of the longest and most boring of all the stories that Hunt gathered. In *Kwakiutl Culture as Reflected in Mythology* Boas termed it "complex": "An inordinate amount of space in this story is taken by the travels of Head-Winter-Dancer and his attempts to get names and privileges by marrying the daughters of chiefs" (Boas 1935:189). The man whose mind is evident in this protracted 1905 text could not have told the taut Asdiwal story we are considering here, any more than Defoe could have written *Tristram Shandy*. Moreover, the 1905 text was, as one would expect, dictated by Ts!oxts!aes in the Native tongue. It is highly unlikely that he could be the source of our story, which Hunt sent initially in English and subsequently offered to translate.

If the above conclusions are correct, we are witnesses here of a subtle interplay between Boas and his chief informant. Hunt, paid by the page, presented an English text taken from a previously published version. Boas, knowing this, kept it back from serious consideration in his comparative work. Then he gave Hunt a chance to explain. But once Hunt had named a source, no matter how preposterous, Boas apparently felt obliged to publish the text in accordance with Hunt's attribution. After Hunt's death in 1933, Boas can state in his final summation in *Kwakiutl Culture as Reflected in Mythology* that the text is "clearly a Tsimshian story retold" (Boas 1935:173), which settles the matter on the side of truth without a hint of anything untoward having happened.

Bibliography

Bibliography

ARCTANDER, JOHN W.
 1909 *The Apostle of Alaska: The Story of William Duncan of Metlakahtla.*
 New York: Fleming H. Revell.

BARBEAU, C. MARIUS
 1917 Review of Tsimshian Mythology. *American Anthropologist*
 19(4):548-563.
 1950 *Totem Poles.* 2 vols. Anthropological Series 30, National Museum
 of Canada Bulletin 119. Ottawa.
 1961 *Tsimsyan Myths.* Anthropological Series 51, National Museum of
 Canada Bulletin 174. Ottawa.

BERMAN, JUDITH
 1991 The Production of the Boas-Hunt Kwakwala Texts. Pp. 1-34 in
 *Papers for the 26th International Conference on Salish and
 Neighbouring Languages.* Vancouver: University of British
 Columbia Press.
 1997 George Hunt and The Social Organization and the Secret Societies
 of the Kwakiutl Indians. Pp. 47-63 in *Papers for the 32nd
 International Conference on Salish and Neighboring Languages.* Port
 Angeles, Washington.

BOAS, FRANZ
 1895 *Indianische Sagen von der nordpacifischen Küste Amerikas.* Berlin: A.
 Asher. Translated in typescript as Indian Myths and Legends from
 the North Pacific Coast of America by Dietrich Bertz for the
 British Columbia Indian Language Project, 1977. Victoria.
 1902 *Tsimshian Texts.* Bureau of American Ethnology Bulletin 27.
 Washington.
 1902 *Kwakiutl Texts.* Memoirs of the American Museum of Natural
 History Vol. 4. New York. (With George Hunt).
 1905 *Kwakiutl Texts.* Publications of the Jesup North Pacific Expedition
 Vol. 3; Memoirs of the American Museum of Natural History Vol.
 5. New York. (With George Hunt).
 1908 Eine Sonnensage der Tsimschian. Zeitschrift für Ethnologie
 40:776-797.

1910 *Kwakiutl Tales.* Columbia Contributions to Anthropology 2. New York.

1911 Tsimshian. Pp. 283-422 in Vol. I of *Handbook of American Indian Languages.* Bureau of American Ethnology Bulletin 40. Washington.

1912 *Tsimshian Texts* (New Series). Publications of the American Ethnological Society 3:65-285. Leyden, The Netherlands: E.J. Brill

1916 *Tsimshian Mythology.* Based on Texts Recorded by Henry W. Tate. Pp. 29-1037 in 31st Annual Report of the Bureau of American Ethnology for the Years 1909-1910. Washington.

1921 Ethnology of the Kwakiutl (Based on Data Collected by George Hunt). Pp. 43-1481 in *35th Annual Report of the Bureau of American Ethnology for the Years 1913-1914.* Washington.

1935 *Kwakiutl Culture as reflected in Mythology.* Memoirs of the American Folk-Lore Society 28. New York.

BOLT, CLARENCE
1992 *Thomas Crosby and the Tsimshian: Small Shoes for Feet Too Large.* Vancouver: University of British Columbia Press.

BRINGHURST, ROBERT
1999 *A Story as Sharp as a Knife: The Classical Haida Mythtellers and Their World.* Vancouver: Douglas and McIntyre.

CAMPBELL, BRAD C.
1975 The Shining Youth in Tsimshian Mytholgy. Pp. 3-26 in *The Tsimshian: Images of the Past, Views for the Present.* Margaret Seguin, ed. Vancouver: University of British Columbia Press.

COLE, DOUGLAS
1999 *Franz Boas: The Early Years, 1858-1906.* Vancouver: Douglas and McIntyre; Seattle: University of Washington Press.

CROSBY, THOMAS
1914 *Up and Down the North Pacific Coast by Canoe and Mission Ship.* Toronto: The Missionary Society of the Methodist Church.

DUFF, WILSON
1959 *Histories, Territories, and Laws of the Kitwancool.* Anthropology in British Columbia Memoir 4. Victoria: British Columbia Provincial Museum.

DUNN, JOHN A.
1978 *A Practical Dictionary of the Coast Tsimshian Language.* National Museum of Man. Mercury Series. Ethnology Service Papers 42. Ottawa.

ELLIS, DAVID W., WITH SOLOMON WILSON.
1980 The Haida Story of Sea Lion Village: The Supreme Power Who Walked About Naked. The Haida Story of the Woman Who Was Kidnapped by the Killer Whales. *The Charlottes* 5:4-9. Skidgate: Queen Charlotte Islands Museum.
1981 *The Knowledge and Usage of Marine Invertebrates by the Skidegate Haida People of the Queen Charlotte Islands.* Skidegate: The Queen Charlotte Islands Museum Society Monograph Series 1.

FREEMAN, DEREK
1966 *Margaret Mead and Samoa: The Making and Unmaking of an Anthropological Myth.* Cambridge: Harvard University Press; Canberra: Australian National University Press.
1999 *The Fateful Hoaxing of Margaret Mead: A Historical Analysis of Her Samoan Research.* Boulder: Westview.

FREEMAN, JOHN F.
1966 *A Guide to Manuscripts Relating to the American Indian in the Library of the American Philosophical Society.* Philadelphia: American Philosophical Society.

GARFIELD, VIOLA E.
1939 *Tsimshian Clan and Society.* University of Washington Publications in Anthropology 7(3):167-340. Seattle.
1953 Contemporary Problems of Folklore Collecting and Study. *Alaska University Anthropological Papers* Vol. I. Pp. 25-36.

HALPIN, MARJORIE M.
1973 The Tsimshian Crest System: A Study Based on Museum Specimens and the Marius Barbeau and William Beynon Field Notes. Ph.D. Dissertation in Anthropology, University of British Columbia, Vancouver.

HALPIN, MARJORIE M. AND MARGARET SEGUIN
1990 Tsimshian Peoples: Southern Tsimshian, Coast Tsimshian, Nishga, and Gitksan. Pp. 267-284 in Northwest Coast, Vol 7 of the *Handbook of North American Indians.* Washington: Smithsonian Institution.

HEALEY, ELIZABETH
1958 *History of Alert Bay District.* Vancouver: J.M. Bow for the Alert Bay Centennial Committee.

HILTON, SUSANNA, JOHN C. RATH, AND EVELYN W. WINDSOR, EDS.
1982 *Oowekeeno Oral Traditions as Told by the Late Chief Simon Walkus, Sr.* National Museum of Man. Mercury Series. Ethnology Service Papers 84. Ottawa.

HYMES, DELL H.
1981 *"In vain I tried to tell you": Essays in Native American Ethnopoetics.* Philadelphia: University of Pennsylvania Press.

JACOBS, MELVILLE
1959 Folklore. Pp. 119-138 in *The Anthropology of Franz Boas: Essays on the Centennial of His Birth.* Memoirs of the American Anthropological Association 89. Menasha, Wisconsin.

LÉVI-STRAUSS, CLAUDE
1967 The Story of Asdiwal. Pp. 1-47 in *The Structural Study of Myth and Totemism.* A.S.A. Monographs 5. London: Tavistock Publications.

MACDONALD, GEORGE F. AND JOHN J. COVE
1987 *Tsimshian Narratives 2.* Canadian Museum of Civilization. Mercury Series Directorate Paper 3. Ottawa.

MAUD, RALPH
1978 *The Salish People: The Local Contribution of Charles Hill-Tout.* 4 Vols. Vancouver: Talonbooks.
1982 *A Guide to B.C. Indian Myth and Legend: A Short History of Myth-collecting and a Survey of Published Texts.* Vancouver: Talonbooks.
1989 The Henry Tate-Franz Boas Collaboration on Tsimshian Mythology. *American Ethnologist* 16(l):158-162.
1993 *The Porcupine Hunter and other Stories: The Original Tsimshian Texts of Henry W. Tate.* Vancouver: Talonbooks.
1998 Tate, Henry Wellington. Pp. 988-999 in *Dictionary of Canadian Biography* 14. Toronto: University of Toronto Press.

MCILWRAITH, THOMAS F.
1948 *The Bella Coola Indians.* 2 Vols. Toronto: University of Toronto Press.

PRICE, ROBIN

1983 *An Annotated Catalogue of Medical Americana in the Library of the Wellcome Institute for the History of Medicine.* London: The Wellcome Institute for the History of Medicine.

RATH, JOHN C.

1992 Notes on Boas-Hunt's North Wakashan Text Materials. *Papers for the 27th International Conference on Salish and Neighboring Languages.*

RIDLEY, WILLIAM

1895 A Grammar of the Zimshian Language, with Some Observations on the People. Manuscript 1812-b in the National Anthropological Archives, Smithsonian Institution, Washington.

1903 *Snapshots from the North Pacific.* London: Church Missionary Society.

ROHNER, RONALD P.

1969 *The Ethnology of Franz Boas: Letters and Diaries of Franz Boas Written on the Northwest Coast from 1886 to 1931.* Chicago: University of Chicago Press.

SPIER, LESLIE

1931 Historical Interrelation of Cultural Traits: Franz Boas's Study of Tsimshian Mythology. Pp. 449-457 in *Methods in Social Science: A Case Book.* Chicago: University of Chicago Press.

STOCKING, GEORGE W., JR.

1989 *A Franz Boas Reader: The Shaping of American Anthropology 1883-1911.* Chicago: University of Chicago Press Midway reprint. Originally Basic Books 1974.

TEDLOCK, DENNIS

1972 *Finding the Center: Narrative Poetry of the Zuni Indians.* New York: The Dial Press.

1977 Toward an Oral Poetics. *New Literary History* 8(3): 507-519. Charlottesville, Virginia.

TEIT, JAMES

1898 *Traditions of the Thompson Indians of British Columbia.* Pp. 1-136 in Memoirs of the American Folk-Lore Society 6. New York.

TOELKEN, BARRE
1981 With Tacheeni Scott. Poetic Retranslation and the "Pretty Languages" of Yellowman. Pp. 65-116 in *Traditional Literatures of the American Indian: Texts and Interpretations*. Lincoln: University of Nebraska Press.

WELLS, OLIVER N.
1987 *The Chilliwacks and their Neighbours*. Vancouver: Talonbooks.